connections

jeremy p. tarcher/penguin

a member of penguin group (usa) inc.

new york

# connections

the five threads of intuitive wisdom

gabrielle roth

Most Tarcher/Penguin books are available at special quantity discounts for bulk purchase for sales promotions, premiums, fund-raising, and educational needs. Special books or book excerpts also can be created to fit specific needs. For details, write Penguin Group (USA) Inc. Special Markets, 375 Hudson Street, New York, NY 10014.

Credits and permissions appear on pp. 179–180.

Jeremy P. Tarcher/Penguin
a member of
Penguin Group (USA) Inc.
375 Hudson Street
New York, NY 10014
www.penguin.com

Library of Congress Cataloging-in-Publication Data

Roth, Gabrielle, date.
    Connections : the 5 threads of intuitive wisdom / by Gabrielle Roth.
        p.   cm
    ISBN 1-58542-327-0 (alk. paper)
1. Intuition. 2. Self-actualization (Psychology) I. Title.
    BF315.5.R68 2004            2004046023

Printed in the United States of America
10  9  8  7  6  5  4  3  2  1

This book is printed on acid-free paper. ∞

BOOK DESIGN BY MEIGHAN CAVANAUGH

to jonathan

beloved son,
keeper of the flame

## acknowledgments

I have the coolest publisher. Joel Fotinos rocks. He inspired this book and gracefully and patiently guided it and me through the process. I thank him and my lovable and loyal agent, Candice Fuhrman, for being so fully present for me whenever I needed them.

For my editors, I fall on my knees. They lifted me out of the dark ten thousand times. I am deeply grateful to Linda Kahn and Hal Bennet. Linda began and ended this journey with me, and although we never left my couch, we traversed many lands of mystery. Her craft was crucial to the destiny of this book as were her wit and wisdom. Hal Bennet met me in the middle and through endless, long-distance conversations and drafts informed this project with poetry and passion. And big thanks to Robert Ansell, my sweet man, who tirelessly (well almost) read, edited, typed, and tap-danced across every page of every draft.

Many amazing people offered their art, creativity, and stories. I especially want to thank: Hans Li, for once again seducing icons out of the dark; Jewel Mathieson, for her badass poetry;

Jonathan Horan, for living the medicine life and sharing himself fearlessly and generously, not to mention for keeping me real on the way.

And I couldn't have made this journey without my posse and several strangers: Donna Karan, soul sister, for carrying me across the great water, over and over again, turning me on to yoga and to my amazing yoga teacher, Rodney Yee; Terry Iacuzzo, my shamanic buddy; Johnny Dark, closet mystic; Lynn Kohlman, warrior babe; Eliezer Sobel, Zen man; Lorca Simons, rock star; Bobby Bethea, trusting soul; Robby Anton, savage angel; Marty Klein, edgewalker; Martha and Zeet Peabody, electric muses; Muireann O'Callaghan, relentless researcher. And to Jared Pitman, my seatmate on United Flight 10 from LAX to JFK, whose innocence and curiosity broke through my writer's block.

And I want to thank The Moving Center road warriors for always being ready to give, to serve, to sacrifice, and to soar—Kathy Altman, Susannah Darling Khan, Ya'Acov Darling Khan, Jonathan Horan, Andrea Juhan, and Lori Saltzman. Indeed, my gratitude includes all of my students—each having been a catalyst for deepening my awareness.

And, at Tarcher/Penguin, huge thanks to Terri Hennessy for her joyful, fun approach to editing as well as for her help in making sure the book made it through the system—no easy task; Meredith Phebus for her production wizardry; and Mitch Horowitz for his enthusiasm and support.

# contents

Let it be for you a great and high mystery in the light of nature that a thing can completely lose and forfeit its form and shape, only to arise subsequently out of nothing and become something whose potency and virtue is far nobler than what it was at the beginning.

PARACELSUS

Your art is the Holy Ghost blowing through
your soul.

JACK KEROUAC

---

**t**wenty years ago I embarked on a search for the perfect
place to live in Manhattan. For seven months I traipsed from
one side of the island to the other, looking at apartments,
townhouses, lofts, even vacant churches. I think I drove my Re-
altor to a support group. One day after looking at an apartment in the Village we got stuck on a one-way street. I looked
out the window and saw a scrap of paper taped to the door of
a building. Something made me hop out of the car. It was ad-
vertising a loft for rent upstairs, on the fifth floor. I rang the
buzzer and the owner showed me the place. The minute I
crossed the threshold I knew I was home.

A friend of mine had been skiing for a week in Aspen. Just

when he was scheduled to go home, a huge storm was predicted, one that would leave a foot of fresh powder. He had no pressing reason to go home—he was single and self-employed—but for some odd reason he boarded the plane, which was the last one to get out. Back in the city, he went to his cousin's birthday party. At 1:00 a.m. he put on his coat to leave, and his cousin said, "You can't leave without meeting my friend." She introduced them, and they talked for two hours. Within a month they were looking for an apartment together and within a year they were married.

An investment banker I know was lying in bed one morning, feeling wretched with a high fever, contemplating taking the day off. But something compelled him to pop some Tylenol and drag himself to the office. He made a deal that day that transformed his entire career.

Coincidence? Miracles? Divine intervention? Are these just once-in-a-lifetime occurrences, things that happen totally unpredictably, once in a blue moon? Or can you live your life on this mysterious, magical wavelength all the time, secure in the knowledge of who you are, where you're going, and how you're going to get there without agonizing and obsessing over every decision? Well, you can; it's just a matter of liberating your soul to follow its true path, using intuition—that holy spark of divine wisdom—as its guide.

Once you awaken your intuition and get in the habit of listening to and acting on it, every decision in your life, be it what to order in a restaurant or whether to take a new job, get married, get pregnant, or join an ashram, will become reflexive and reflective of your inner truth. The trick is not to try to work out all the answers in your head. Rather, take whatever information you need into your body, trust your gut, then dance or meditate or walk or do whatever you do to enter a really relaxed state of being, and you'll know what to do. You always have and you always will.

A friend of mine has just been diagnosed with breast cancer. One of her options is a mastectomy, the other is to watch and wait. Her surgeon suggested that she take a couple of weeks to not think about it. He said, "Go home and have some fun. Deep down you already know what you need to do. Thinking about it—forcing a decision—will only cause anxiety and eventually regret. In a week or two, you'll simply know what to do." And she did.

Imagine if we could go through life always knowing what to do or not to do! Actually, we do, but we don't trust this inner wisdom as often as we could. Living intuitively enables us to read subtle shifts in people's vibes, to distinguish among fear, fantasies, and genuine danger, and to know which direction to go when faced with a fork in the road. It's about distinguishing who you are from who you aren't and finding where your idiosyncratic personal truth merges with the greater truth of the universe. It's a way of being.

Each of us comes into the world 100 percent intuitive; it's just a matter of reclaiming your birthright. To do that you need to get out of your own way, to strip away the things that are blocking, distracting, diffusing, suppressing, and depressing the natural dance of your intuition.

The purpose of getting in touch with your intuition is not to perform, to dazzle, to distinguish yourself as more talented or exciting or tuned in than anyone else. On the contrary, being in touch with your intuition is the most humbling experience I know. Instead of helping you aggrandize yourself, it abnegates the self, and you become a vessel, a channel, a tool. The highest purpose of intuition is to serve your higher self and the higher self of others, and in serving others to experience the mysterious wisdom of the soul.

To fully realize our intuitive abilities we need to be instinctive, intimate, intent, integral, and inspired. Each of these energies is a facet of intuition, our connection to the divine force that moves all things. The problem happens when we stop trusting its supreme intelligence, when we allow our intuition to be overwhelmed and diminished by the loud, reactive, defensive voices of the ego.

The ego is all about self-importance. Carlos Castaneda's Don Juan calls it a "foreign installation." It has nothing to do with who we really are, where we are going, or how we will get there. Indeed, it can only sabotage any inquiry into what is true, real, and worthy of our attention. The ego wants to define us, hide us, diminish us, separate us, and sabotage us. It lives in the shadows, popping up like a mole every time we reach for something real. It's a guerrilla warrior who leaps out of the jungle and ambushes us as we bushwhack our way toward the lost kingdom.

Our mission is to resist its attacks and keep focused on our ultimate goal—to discover the unique dance by which each of us can best serve humanity.

If intuition is our superhero, our inner Batman, the ego is our inner Joker, constantly scheming our demise and creating roadblocks that prevent us from fulfilling our destiny. To liberate our intuition, we must outsmart our ego.

We come in with an intelligence that is meant to serve the world in some way, and however small or large our contribution, it is our task to discover it. And the fastest way to do this is to become deeply rooted in the mysterious workings of your inner world. For me, being rooted means finding my feet, rocking in the rhythm of the world beat. When we dance, we wake up, we get down and juicy with ourselves, we have fun and forget all the heavy shit we carry around. In the dance we get real, get free, get over ourselves. Movement kicks ass. When you truly surrender to your own rhythm, you look so cool, so mysterious, so seductive—the way you deep down really want to look but don't trust that you do.

I don't think life has any particular meaning beyond our experience of it, and the afterlife is like an afterthought—it comes a bit late. The time to get into your groove is right now. And the way to do it is to get comfortable in the mystery, calm in the dark, centered in chaos, connected to the unified field, and committed to fulfilling your destiny. Being true to the signs and signals that come from within, learning to distinguish between those that come from the soul and those that come from the ego, is our holy work, work that will make us whole. People can do a lot of things for us, but this one thing only we can do for ourselves.

Like a spiderweb, this book is not linear or prescriptive. All its points are interconnected in a very delicate way. Strands of wisdom collected over years of dancing with a tribe of seekers have coalesced into a mystical matrix for you to traverse in your own quest for a soulful existence.

Intuition is your passport to this unseen magical world, which, like the spiderweb below, has five realms. In each of these realms you make an offering. Offer your body to the realm of mystery and receive the gift of instinct. Offer your heart to the realm of darkness and receive the gift of intimacy. Offer your mind to the realm of chaos and receive the gift of intention. Offer your soul to the realm of unity and receive the gift of integrity. Offer your spirit to the realm of destiny and receive the gift of inspiration.

Your challenge will be to keep a wary eye out for your ego, which wants to ensnare you in its own web of self-importance. In the realm of mystery, it will try to define you. In the realm of darkness, it will try to hide you. In the realm of chaos, it will try to diminish you. In the realm of unity, it will try to separate you. In the realm of destiny, it will try to sabotage you. The ego is all about controlling and fixing you so you aren't free to move, to change, or to grow. To dance your dreams, you need to trust your intuition, for your intuition feeds your soul, and your soul is the most essential part of you.

Intuition is a spiritual force, the force that guides and moves you along your spiritual path. It's when our feet, our hands, our breath, our belly are all in service to the Great Spirit. Only when we fully embrace our own intuitive intelligence will our souls be liberated to fulfill their destiny.

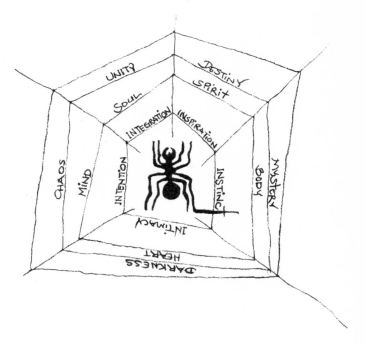

# cruising emptiness

There ain't no answer. There ain't going to be any answer. There never has been an answer. That's the answer.

GERTRUDE STEIN

For sorcerers, discipline is an art; the art of facing infinity without flinching, not because they are filled with toughness, but because they are filled with awe.

CARLOS CASTANEDA (VENTURA)

You are the guardians of God's light, so come return to the root of the root of your own self.

RUMI

## 7 1/2 months pregnant

Questing I have climbed mountains
sat in sacred spots
soaked my brain in substances
danced naked in full in moonlight
walked on hot coals
prayed, prostrated
and chanted mantras until my tongue numbed
but I've never been closer to the mystery
nearer to God than now
in the red velvet recliner
feeling you roll over
and gently drum
from under my skin

JEWEL MATHIESON

tracking inner truth

If you relax, you accept; acceptance of existence
is the only way to relax.

OSHO

**a**t fifteen, I jumped into the back seat of a friend's car,
ready to take off on an excellent adventure with five of my
friends. Suddenly my mother came flying across our front lawn
waving a wooden spoon covered in chocolate icing, yelling,
"Gabrielle, get out of that car. You can't go!" She was banging
on the window of the car, looking absolutely deranged. Morti-
fied, pissed off, and freaked out, I got out of the car. My
friends sped off. I sulked. Several blocks away, a car ran a red
light and smashed into the side of their car, demolishing the
back seat where moments before I had been ready to rock. I
didn't tell my mom what had happened for fear that every time
she got nervous about my plans she'd pull this one out of the

archives. But the whole thing left me stunned, spending many a night lying on my bed staring at the ceiling, pondering the mystery of it all.

My mother's intuitive instincts were part of my reality, embedded in my genetic code, whether I accepted them or not. Knowing things out of the blue scared me, and my psychic flashes freaked other people out, too. They were like no other feelings. They were overwhelming, visceral, kinesthetic, animalistic. It was like being taken over by a huge, primitive force—an inner tidal wave.

A few years later in college, my roommate told me she was going out on a blind double date. There was no logical reason for objecting, but every cell in my body screamed, "Don't go!" No form of persuasion worked. She just laughed and called me an overprotective den mother. All four people were killed in a fatal crash that night.

This completely shook me up and strung me out. How was it possible to know what was going to happen to another human being? This wasn't a mother's instinct. What did this mean about the future if it could be felt before it happened? Was I somehow responsible for her death? Could I have prevented it? These questions tore me apart.

At some point it became clear that what was going on was so much bigger than anything I could figure out, it left me with two choices: either drive myself crazy or surrender to my gut instincts—not analyze them but respect their mysterious flow.

Instinct is the intuition of the body. It's very primal—you

might break out in a sweat or chills, find yourself pacing or paralyzed when you know that you or someone dear to you, or even a total stranger, is in danger. Sensing danger, my entire body gets very still, and only my head moves. I feel like a light-house, sending a beam across the murky waters in eerie still-ness. Suddenly, my beam stops and focuses, and in that instant I receive a directive telling me exactly what I am dealing with. Hands have told me they wanted to kill somebody, and the ocean has told me it was about to devour my house.

On a less dramatic level, following your instincts might lead you to make a seemingly offhand decision like getting off the bus a stop early or not enrolling your kid in a school you had your heart set on. Eating lunch with a friend in a restaurant, just after we'd been served our food, I had the absolute instinct to change tables immediately. Five minutes after we moved, the chandelier crashed on our original table. As Woody Allen said, "The next time God tests me, I hope he gives me a written."

Basically, instinct bypasses the brain, grabs the body, and lets you know loud and clear what to do or not do. The problem is that when we live in our heads we may not hear or feel our instincts. Or if we do, we may resist following them because we are insulated in a cocoon of identities, personas—images of ourself as someone who acts in a certain way. Say you have a cheap airline ticket to go to a friend's wedding, but for no ap-parent reason your body does not want to get on that plane. You're not scared—it feels more like plain old stubbornness. A battle ensues. Your head tells you that you can't miss the wedding.

What would everybody think? Besides you'll lose the money for the ticket. Meanwhile your gut is screaming, "Don't go!" So what do you do?

Myself, I'd stay home and forget about everyone else's opinions. It's not that the plane will necessarily crash, but there's some reason you weren't meant to go to that wedding. If you trust your instincts above all else, you won't have regrets.

Obsessing over what image you project to other people is a symptom of self-importance and cuts you off from your instincts. In this state of being you think you know all the answers; in fact, you probably think you are the answer. You believe your own PR when in reality it's just a puff piece. And the one blowing the hot air is your ego. It hates ambiguity and wants you to be attached to a particular concept or notion of who you are.

But identity is merely a paperweight, one of those gifts people give when they can't think of what to give. Something to pin us down, to keep us from moving like light, like air, like rhythm. The challenge is to drop the baggage of identity, with its past and probable futures. We need to let go of fixed ideas, behaviors, attachments. Yes, it's scary, but the payoff is being that mysterious utterly fascinating self you know deep down you are. Unfettered, your true self flows to the surface and moves you toward your purpose, your destiny here on this earth.

Living by your instincts is living in the mystery. It requires total surrender to the unknown. It's like walking in water. You step into the current with nothing to hold on to, and it washes you clean like a baptism, purging away any fixed images you have of yourself and freeing you to be the divine self you are destined to be.

## the route of the root

The moon lives in the lining of your skin.
PABLO NERUDA, *Love*

As I arrived at the dance studio last weekend, Sanga, drummer extraordinaire, was nonchalantly leaning against the brick wall in his canary yellow boots—not knowing, of course, that on that very morning in the Sunday Styles section of *The New York Times*, canary yellow was mentioned as the new "It" color. Some people are born cool. I hugged him and continued my cell-phone conversation.

"Everybody's walking their talk," Sanga said. I looked around and counted seven others cell to ear. Probably not what the Native Americans had in mind when they coined the phrase.

It seems like the whole western world is suffering from an information overload. My husband blames it on the advent of the remote. Since the cable man handed him the clicker, he has had the attention span of a four-year-old. He's constantly switching among five hundred channels because he's afraid he's missing something, and when he's not watching TV, he's checking his e-mail, his voice-mail, or his inner to-do lists. People exhibit the same behavior in their relationships. We are not paying attention, not to ourselves, not to each other, not to what's going on around us.

Of course, we can't stop the world, unplug all our modems and devices, and go back to candlelight and horse-drawn buggies. We have to accept the speed and rhythm of our times and yet realize that the more potential we have to be distracted, the more urgently we need to be grounded. Cavemen didn't worry about being grounded because their lives revolved around the earth and the immediate needs of their bodies. But the more sophisticated we've become, the more mental stimulation we've required, the more disconnected we've become from our bodies and the earth.

Our bodies, however, are the root of our true selves, the home of our souls. Our desire to constantly change and control our bodies indicates a deep distrust of our souls. We try the latest diets, the latest treatments, the latest implants in a desperate effort to hold back the tides of change, to fix our bodies in an eternally pubescent state.

But in denying our bodies' natural processes we deny their earthy, sensual source of wisdom. Not the kind of wisdom you'll find in the library, but a spontaneous, instinctive wisdom that illuminates the present moment. Being aware of this wisdom passing through our physical selves keeps us grounded and connected to everything happening around us, in tune with the vibrations of the universe.

Animals operate on this sensory, vibratory wavelength—just think about how dogs bark before an earthquake or how flocks of birds or schools of fish move in perfect formation. We have the potential to be just as incisive and aware, because the truth is that we're animals. Ninety-nine percent of our DNA is virtually identical to the genome of a lab mouse.

Consider a TV show I just saw about a cat with real street smarts. A British family lived in Swansea—parents, college-aged son and daughter, two cats, and a dog. The parents moved to Bath and left behind their kids, who were going to college in Swansea. They took all the pets, including Sooty, a black cat who was especially close to the children. After a few days in Bath, Sooty disappeared. Six months later, Sooty showed up in Swansea at the home of the kids. The trip would have been more than one hundred miles if it were all overland, and more than sixty miles if she had found one of two bridges that crossed the river. Moreover, the kids had since moved to a different flat in Swansea, and Sooty found them there.

We can't crawl on all fours or lick our bodies the way cats do. Our ability to think is a wonderful thing. We can imagine, create, even make fun of ourselves. It's just that thinking and knowing are different, and knowing comes from a more primitive wisdom, a timeless connection to the movement, to the dance of the universe and all its beings. Imagine you have an inner black cat prowling your field of dreams.

The concept of evolution as a progression toward an ideal of perfection may simply be a judgment. We may be moving away from something perfectly essential, not just toward something essentially perfect. Evolution could be devolution. Progress could be regress. Unless we value our feet as much as our frontal lobes, we'll end up as disembodied talking heads with no rhythm, no root.

Years ago, a friend gave me a capsule filled with a brown, powdery substance he called Ibogane, a root from Africa. I took it, at night, sitting on a wide flat rock in the back mountains of Big Sur. I felt at one with my whole environment, part of the rock, the sky, the wind. At some point in my journey, a mountain lion appeared, walked around my rock, and stood next to it for a long time. I had no fear of this she-lion, never entertained the thought that I might be her dinner. We were two beings resonating on the same vibratory level. The next day I thought perhaps I had hallucinated this cat. But her tracks were all around the rock.

It's on this vibrational, instinctive level that you tap into your animal magnetism, the stuff that makes you irresistible, fascinating, charismatic, sexy—all the stuff you project onto a Victoria's Secret miracle bra. Once, as part of a casting process, I auditioned eight hundred actor/dancers, many of whom had been in a major Broadway musical. Oddly, one of the six I chose had never danced in his life, but when he moved from one side of the stage to the other I couldn't take my eyes off him. That's animal magnetism. Without grounding in our bodies, we're like lightning, occasionally destructive, most often dissipated in a flash. To harness our power, we need to enter the deep dark of our bodies and truly become "guardians of god's light."

My three-and-a-half-year-old friend Elliot was painting a rainbow recently, and as he dipped his paintbrush into the brown he asked his dad if rainbows have brown in them. His dad said no, so he immediately drew a root on his rainbow.

We all need to be like rooted rainbows, simultaneously earthy and etheric. It's great to gaze at the stars as long as you feel your feet on the ground.

## fire-breathing dragons

We don't know
We just don't know
Whether the shoe drops in the morning
or an astronaut wears it to the moon
SAPPHIRE

As soon as you have it all figured out, or are finally convinced you can't, life will surely test you. It's all part of living with the Mystery.

One day you're walking along thinking you have some idea of what your life is about and—wham. The universe throws you down, and you realize that you don't know shit.

October 2 was that kind of day. It started out with tea and toast, reading the *Times,* then proceeded into errand duty. At

4:30 p.m., I had two things left on my list—plan my European itinerary with the travel agent and get a routine chest x-ray. There wasn't time to do both, so I chose the travel agent and began walking down Fifth Avenue. But when I crossed Twelfth Street, I abruptly made a right turn in the direction of the hospital.

Arriving at 4:45 was an inspired move. It was Friday afternoon, and everybody wanted to get out of there by 5:00. For the first time, there was no waiting. I soon found myself sitting in a tiny, closet-like room with the nurse, the same woman who's done my X-rays for several years. It's doubtful she recognized me; to her, I'm just another chest, whereas to me she is a Slavic princess. After the chest X-ray, I returned to my closet to wait for her to tell me I could get dressed. Instead she returned and said, "We need to take another slide. Don't worry."

Her telling me not to worry was worrisome. After the second X-ray, she told me to get dressed. I saw something hidden in the shadows of her face. A cold wind had blown through her, and instead of standing three feet apart it was as if we were standing on distant sides of an abyss.

The abyss was in my belly. It was cold and gray, and I knew my mind was not meant to wander there. Yet my ego was screaming with worst-case scenarios.

*Om Mane Padme Hum.*

Have you ever been stranded on the border between faith and fear, waiting for a doctor to return your call and tell you what you already know but can't quite comprehend? The radiologist had noted a dark spot on my lung. As Vladimir said in *Waiting for Godot,* "Things have changed here since yesterday."

Over the next several days, every part of me was tested: brain, bone, blood. No evidence of cancer was found, but surgery was still advised. I went to a top guy on the recommendation of a friend. He matter-of-factly described the twenty-inch scar, the six-month recovery, the possibility of death. I kept staring at his hands. I couldn't imagine them in my body. Indeed, my body contracted instinctively away from him. I didn't trust him.

It took four weeks to get a doctor to give me a second opinion. He'd come with no recommendation; it was simply a matter of timing. I needed to see someone, and when I called the hospital, he was the only one available. Luck of the draw. He described a totally different procedure—three half-inch scars, a six-week recovery, an optimistic prognosis. His long, delicate fingers fluttered in the air as he spoke, almost taking wing, communicating a sensitivity. The message from my inner sanctum was that my body was open, relaxed. I trusted him. So we scheduled the operation.

Surgery is a dark place. Indeed, the anesthesia is like a shaman's trance, transporting us to a space beyond time until the job is done and we drift back to a world that we know.

The recovery room, by contrast, is a bright place. Out of the darkness into the light. Men and women in green and white doing the slow-motion hustle amid patients, machines, IV drips.

Kathy, my nurse, plugged me into my Walkman. Sufi trance music whirled in my ears. Kathy handed me a plastic tube with a tiny yellow ball inside and told me to breathe into it. When I could get the ball up to a certain point, I'd be allowed to leave the recovery room. Before I had a chance to prove my prowess a doctor and several nurses clustered around my gurney. One felt my pulse while the others stared at a machine behind my head. They looked worried. I asked Kathy, "What's going on?"

"Your blood pressure is falling," she said calmly.

"Can you find me some rock and roll?"

"I'll try," she replied, and went on the hunt. She returned with a CD. "Gloria Estefan is all I could find."

"Perfect. Plug me in."

I willed my heart to go with Gloria's beat. Her song pulsed through me. I felt it in every part of me—my hands, my butt, the soles of my feet. Gloria was in my ear singing, "Rhythm is gonna get you." And I believed. Before the song was over, my blood pressure was back to its normal low, and soon afterward I was rolling down the hallway to my room—in the company of Sister Morphine. I surrendered to the world behind my eyes, the space between my bones, as the world slipped away from me. The sun went down, and I went with it.

My lung thing turned out okay. Just a microscopic piece of benign dead tissue. The doctors still don't know what caused it. In spite of the horror, fear, and pain, I learned a lot from the surgery. It took me to my edge, to the crack between worlds where I could see myself waving goodbye to me. And it showed me that I had the inner strength to will myself back. Or maybe I was just freaked out at the thought of dying in that shabby green gown and spending my last moments under bright lights on that uncomfortable gurney, surrounded by strangers.

The biggest lesson I learned is that apart from the gown, surgery isn't that different from everyday life. Most of us spend a great deal of our time anesthesized. Sure, we may go through the motions, but we do so unconsciously, as if we were sleep-walking. We're there—in the office, on the subway, in the bar, at dinner, at the gym—in body but not in soul. Our awareness has been tranquilized by our ego, which has a vested interest in keeping us down under, asleep to our dreams. In some cases, the ego literally drugs us into an alcoholic, chocaholic, work-aholic, or shopaholic daze. In other cases, it hypnotizes us into a narrow-minded little trance—the supermom trance, the obsessive romantic trance, the fame-and-fortune trance, the keeping-up-with-the-neighbors trance. In any case, it etherizes our aware-ness, our sense of living consciously and being present in the moment. It suffocates our soul.

Why do we allow this to happen? Because being entranced by the ego prevents us from feeling pain; in fact, it prevents us from feeling anything—ecstasy, grief, compassion, anger, shame, love—from feeling alive.

Instincts are like guardian angels. Picture Gabriel with his trumpet, sounding us out of our reverie. Instincts know what we need and when we need it. They are the part of us that overrides our hyperconscious, ego-inflated heads and takes the wheel when we're unconscious. In this case, my guardian angel knew whose hands to put me in and that I needed some intravenous rock and roll when I hit rock bottom. And even though being in a body has been my greatest struggle on this earth, when tested, I trusted my body, trusted my instincts, my will to live. Staring down death is a confidence builder.

Movement practice is all about uncovering long-suppressed instincts. It trains you to see with your third eye and listen with your third ear. In testy moments, we need a practice, something to fall back on, a pipeline to our inner truth, or we will find ourselves helpless, surrendering to the will of our heads, not our guts.

On the radio last night a Tibetan monk was saying that each morning, before you get up, you should just lie there for a moment and enjoy the warmth of your body. You should scan from head to toe, noticing how each part feels. You can do that at any time during the day; it never gets boring because we are constantly changing. That's what keeps us mysterious. That's what keeps us alive.

# the chiffon man

In this world of trickery, emptiness is what your soul wants.
RUMI

It's taken thousands of years of stargazing for us to let go of the myth—the fantasy—that we will ever truly understand the universe or ourselves. The greatest physicists willingly admit that at heart we are all part of the mystery. Unfortunately, when it comes to our inner universe, we still believe that if we try hard enough and look deep enough we'll find a finite answer to the question of who we are. But, let's face it, the essence of who we are is the greatest mystery of all, not a simple puzzle to be solved, like the daily crossword.

Every Tuesday, flipping open the science section of the paper, I'm amazed at the discoveries being made about the human body. While it's wonderful that diseases can be cured, organs can be transplanted, ovaries can be frozen, noses can be fixed, and fat can be vacuumed like a living room carpet, the fact of the matter is we remain in the dark about the spark of life that animates our bodies. We're spending billions to decode human DNA, but in the end, what will it give us but a laundry list of proteins? Knowing the chemicals that make me up doesn't get me any closer to knowing who I am.

Once upon a time I was sitting on a red zafu staring into the left eye of a friend, also on a zafu, doing a meditation called *trespasso.* A simple white candle flickered in the space between us. We had been doing this meditation with different partners for four hours every day for several weeks. It was a fall night in Manhattan, and below me the traffic zoomed on Central Park West. The hum of the city buzzed through me. I sank deeper into my breath, into my friend's eye, and suddenly I was staring at the wall behind him, staring right through his body, which looked absolutely diaphanous, barely visible. The small Thangka with Green Tara that hung directly behind him on the wall was clearly visible to me. He was a curious combination of light and void.

A sense of wonder shot through me, and I clung to my breath, refusing any thoughts, trying to enjoy it as long as possible. It was only afterward, when I tried to integrate this milestone into the world of steaming coffee and the sweet scent of Star Gazers on the table behind me, that I reencountered my ever-rational ego, ready to shatter and disdain any experience that it couldn't grasp.

When Carlos Castaneda visualized people's essence, he saw blue eggs. Being a fashion junkie, I saw chiffon—a chiffon man. All I perceived was his energy, not the weight of his life. And in his emptiness he was absolutely luminous. He was simply space. Thinking back on this blissful experience, it's surprising I ever returned to life as we know it. Funny, we're always complaining that we need more space, and yet, in truth, all we are is space.

The great mystery of the body is that it's an apparition. Imagine if we really allowed that fact into our consciousness!

What would happen to all those helpful women behind the makeup counter at Saks? Who needs makeup once you realize you're making the whole thing up?

If there's one thing that decades of dancing have taught me, it is that there is another way to think about the body that has nothing to do with genes or cholesterol levels. It is to see the body as an energy field.

At beginning of my workshops, heaviness often hangs over the room. It's as though everyone were standing there with huge rocks in their pockets. How weighed down they are by their memories, disappointments, losses, stresses, fears, beliefs—all the extra burdens they don't need to be carrying. But they don't know that yet. After a couple of hours of dancing, the room looks different. There's more space and bodies feel lighter. It's not that they've been burning off pounds, although that may very well happen, too. It's psychological weight they've lost. Where once the energy of their bodies was dense and static, it's now flowing and light, fluid and glistening.

It's hard to let go of the idea that the body is solid and fixed—not to mention that it's an important part of one's identity. Especially these days, when we're so overinvested in our physical appearance, running from the gym to the manicurist to the spa. While taking care of our bodies is important for our health and mental well-being, never forget that the body is merely a vessel for the soul. By itself, it has very little to do with who we really are.

We're not only obsessive but possessive about our bodies.

This is me, this is my body, *mi casa*. However, we don't often regard *mi casa* as *tu casa*. In actuality it isn't just yours or mine, it's an ancestral estate. Maybe you have your great-grandmother's eyes, your Uncle Izzie's head for numbers, or your father's slump. You're just a way station as these qualitites, energies, and shapes continue their journey into the next generation.

Physicists are now realizing that the body is "emptiness and rhythm. At the ultimate heart of the body, at the heart of the world, there is no reality. Once again, there is only the dance."* The dance of electrons around protons, the dance of molecules within cells, the dance of blood within veins. We are only energy, the most mysterious force of all.

> If you look at zero you see nothing;
> but look through it and you will see the world.
> ROBERT KAPLAN, *The Nothing That Is*

---

*Mu Soeng, *Heart Sutra: Ancient Buddhist Wisdom in the Light of Quantum Reality* (Cumberland, R.I.: Primary Point Press, 1991), p. 18.

# all or nothing

I went to the doctor. "I feel lost,
blind with love. What should I do?"
Give up owning things and being
somebody. Quit existing.
RUMI

For the past couple of generations, we've been experiment-
ing with all different kinds of ways—both wacky and wonderful—to find ourselves. The core question is not who is the real
me, but why the hell are we asking that question in the first
place? We're desperate to give ourselves labels and titles, yet
petrified that these identities will give the wrong impression.
We're afraid to be seen and afraid not to be seen—equally scared
to be somebody and nobody.

A friend obsessing about someone who'd accused her of being disloyal. She was devastated. "I can't believe it," she said.
"You know me, I'm as loyal as a German shepherd!" She went
on and on.

It was impossible to stay focused on my friend's words. Instead, I found myself tuning in to the two girls at the next table
who were having an animated conversation in Chinese. I didn't
understand a word they were saying, but the tone of their conversation was light and lyrical. My friend's voice was ponderous
and dissonant. I felt like drowning in my latte.

What bothered me so much about my friend? It struck me

that I'd encountered something similar on the dance floor a hundred times before. It had to do with a certain rigidity, a tendency to cling to an inner image of how we want the world to see us. It seems to me there are only two positions worthy of our attention: knowing we are *everything* and knowing we are *nothing*. When we insist on being or not being *something*, that's when the trouble starts.

"I am nothing if not a loyal friend!" my friend screeched, looking absolutely deranged.

I felt so bad—for her, for me, for us. We suffer so much over bullshit.

"It's okay," I whispered. "It really is. None of us is *always* anything. If you can't let that in, you'll never know if you were or weren't loyal."

"Do you really think I'd betray a friend?" she asked, incredulous, making one last stab at getting my reassurance.

"Judas gave betrayal a really bad rap, but we've all done it," I said.

She laughed at the part about Judas and for the time being dropped the subject.

Why it is so difficult to accept that we are *everything*? It's no big secret that any of us can morph into a liar, a lover, or a caring, loyal friend at the flick of a finger. Does a day pass when I don't go through a whole range of attitudes—tender one moment, uptight the next, generous, mean-spirited, guarded, gorgeous, and geeky all rolled into one? Whatever possibilities exist, we have been or will be them, even if only in our heads or hearts. Shape-shifting is a part of being human; maybe it's even what we're here to do and be.

My worst times are when I try to be *something*, like the good-person-who-never-lies-or-wishes-someone-dead, or the woman-who-never-betrays-anyone. How many times have you caught yourself in the act of having to be right or having to be the one who is always wronged; the one who's hip and in the know, or the standard-bearer of traditional values? There's nothing wrong with dropping into those roles in the process of trying to find meaning in the chaos of it all. The problem is, inertia takes hold and keelhauls you through the briny shallows of your own trip. Then you get attached to a particular identity and start being *something*. It's important to know the signs. When part of me squats in the dust with my abacus, counting beads, defining, defending, judging, and justifying my own *something* and comparing it to others' *somethings*—that's when I'm in trouble. Attachment guarantees that you will wake up every morning with a mission: to prove you are who you think you are—today. But it's a total energy drain. You're so busy performing a role that you miss out on the freedom to improvise, to be real rather than rehearsed.

Instead, sit naked and contemplate not the question of your existence but all the answers you've been given, as well as those you've chosen. Take on your identities one by one. Maybe you think you're a dreamer or a loser or a warrior, a lawyer, a great lover, an old fart. Think about who you are according to your father, your mother, different friends, teachers, lovers, and so on. As Bernie Mac says, "If it don't apply, let it fly."

See yourself through as many prisms as you can. Open yourself up to know life's secrets from within the frail wall of skin that is your body from within the chalice of your magic, from within the cloak of your inner mystic. Which images do you readily embrace? Defend? Back away from? Savor each one. Then release each one by imagining this image of yourself floating in a dark sky like a lonely star until it is galaxies removed and reabsorbed back into the universal flow of all things.

We lose ourselves in our strivings to be someone, to build consistency of character. We collude with each other to keep each other small and predictable. But when we open our eyes to see beyond what we want to see, we might discover that the woman in the tall, spike-heeled Manolo Blahnik shoes is really a tightrope walker or high-steel construction worker. And maybe we notice that the Harley coming up in our rearview mirror isn't piloted by a 235-pound truck mechanic with tattoos on his hairy chest and arms but a fragile femme fatale, a mother of two, who, with leathers and helmet and big black boots, has transformed into a badass biker chick. And what about that body builder on your TV? Is he really the elected governor of a state?

Being everything doesn't mean being everything to everybody and nothing to ourselves. We've all had our moments playing out that stereotype—high-spirited and full of energy in public, but drained and empty in the privacy of our boudoir. This is the shadow side of being *everything*, a big bunch of *somethings*—roles and duties and titles, like having a three-page resume, or eighteen letters after your name or luggage in the closet with forty-two stickers on it—been there, going there, anticipating one trip, remembering another, but empty now.

Allowing ourselves to be everything is liberating, not confining; it is endless potential, energy unshackled. It's having the freedom to be who we want to be and the compassion to know that sometimes we can even be okay with being who we don't want to be in spite of our best intentions.

Play with this possibility. If you can accept that you already are *everything*, then you become impossible to define. Indeed, you are *nothing*, and nothing is required to be *nothing*. You can relax a bit, drop your cover, and keep seeking the emptiness. You can start taking refuge in the spaciousness within you, the part that can only be cultivated by meditation, by movement, by dance.

Being *everything* and *nothing* frees us to be instinctive and spontaneous, keys to accessing the mystery. Being *something* locks the door on it, puts you outside the speakeasy with no clue about the password. The paradox of no-self being the real self, of a fluid rather than fixed self—this is liberation.

If you're not the person in your passport photo—the 5-foot 6-inch black-haired, green-eyed person with a mole on your left cheek—then who are you? The only way to find out is to let go, and shift your identity from the dancer to the dance.

# trapped light

The book of moonlight is not written yet.
WALLACE STEVENS

Mystery is everywhere—across the breakfast table in the eyes of the spouse you've known for thirty years, in your kids who will harbor untold surprises, in the features of an elder whose face is lined with stories. But the most mysterious person you'll ever meet is the one in the mirror.

Check yourself out in a full-length mirror, because if you want to experience your mysterious self to the fullest, you'll have to start by becoming aware of your feet. They're not just excuses to buy shoes, they're the route to your root. Finding your feet is the fastest way to get out of your head. Your feet can take you on a journey; your head can only take you on a trip. In the immortal words of Rumi, "your head is the ladder, bring it down under your feet."

I dream all the shoes of my life walking together along a trail, revealing a hidden thread. My shoes know where I've been. They declare my body's history. Each shoe held a dream, from my shiny, black Mary Janes glistening with Vaseline to my scuffed-up army-issue combat boots. From my pink satin toe shoes to my hand-tooled alligator cowboy boots. From my Maud Frizon silver mules to my battered black jazz shoes.

But what's more important than the shoes is the feet that wear them. Feet on earth know. What I've sought all my life through dance is an intimate conversation with the earth, with something bigger than myself. My feet caress the skin of the divine mother. The vibrations they pick up are her secrets revealing themselves to me. It is this connection with the mystery, the dark feminine, the Divine Source from which the spirit of life is born.

To enter the mystery you have to do a striptease, including kicking off the stilettos. Peel away layers of invented and inherited selves. With each consecutive skin you shed you lighten up, let go of control, and become more fluid and fascinating— even to yourself. That very self that doesn't even exist except as a dance, a field of energy.

As Heisenberg said in his uncertainty principles, you can't measure a particle's momentum and position at the same time because particles are always in motion. The self is the same way. The self is a dance, constantly in motion. Any time we try to measure it's position by pinning it down and defining it, we destroy it. So the uncertainty that we are struggling against is the nature of the beast.

In its uncertainty and fluidity, the self is utterly fascinating. Imagine how boring you would be if you never changed, if you were frozen in time with the same heroes, hairdos, and heartaches. Imagine if you were still doing the same dance you did in high school. Still obsessing over the same issues; still bullied by the same beliefs; still making the same choice, safety or stardom, Jesus or James Brown, Virgin Mary or Bloody Mary.

Release yourself from old attachments and baggage. Cross off the people on your Christmas card list that you don't even like or speak to. Give away clothes from your skinny days, your fat days, your punk phase or one shopping craze or another. And then there are all those tchotchkes. Your beer stein collection, the stolen shot glasses, Aunt Tilly's figurines. Empty the drawer of business cards with god-knows-whose phone numbers scrawled on the back. Throw out unfinished projects or journals, recipes you'll never try, back issues of magazines you'll never read. Set up shop on eBay. Someone out there is dying to pay for your karma. Once you've stripped your environment of all those reminders of past selves, you'll find their hold on you decreases. Your surroundings should reflect who you are now.

It's amazing how lightly we can travel if we whittle ourselves down to the bare essentials—inner and outer. But for some reason, we are compelled to schlep the past with us wherever we go. I refer back to my closet, the me that says to another me: "But what if I need one brown boot someday? Maybe I'll go to a Halloween party as a half-wit."

The fastest, cleanest, most joyful way to break out of your own box is by dancing. I'm not talking about doing the stand-and-sway. I'm talking about dancing so deep, so hard, so full of the beat that you are nothing but the dance and the beat and the sweat and the heat. This uninhibited, spontaneous, unchoreographed way of dancing is like leaping from a plane without a parachute. Sure, you have a little ego death. But don't worry, your ego has mastered the resurrection thing. It'll be back.

Dance is movement, is action, and like all action, it reveals us to ourselves in the doing. You know the times you're out there dancing, recycling your basic moves, while you're a million miles away. You're "doing" your dance. Suddenly, Spirit whacks you, takes over your body and all kinds of moves break out. You teeter on the edge, between the known and the unknown, slip into the mystery, allow yourself to be blown away. Now the dance is "doing" you. You are *being* the dance, following your instincts into your groove. There is a spiritual force driving your dance, that strips you to your naked soul.

Surrendering to movement practice teaches us to trust. When you dance, you experience God, that fierce force, the energy that is the universe. Its power, its infinite wisdom, become part of you. In these moments, I don't think, I *know* that there is something beautiful and good and loving underpinning everyone and everything.

That's not to say that dancing on this earth isn't going to cause us its own kind of pain. As we move in the Mystery, we have to offer all of ourselves back to the dance, and there's room for blisters, wounds, and healing there. Take it from Rumi: "Dancing is not rising to your feet painlessly like a whirl of dust blown about by the wind. Dancing is when you rise above both worlds, tearing your heart to pieces and giving up your soul."

The Tao, the energy that moves all things, teaches us to be like water, to flow without resistance, to trust that the process will take us wherever we need to go. We need to let go of all our security blankets—physical, psychological, political—and just be. We need to topple the fortress of fixed ideas, personas, and agendas walling us off from our own two feet and the earth they walk on.

# dancing in the dark

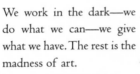

We work in the dark—we
do what we can—we give
what we have. The rest is the
madness of art.
HENRY JAMES, *The Middle Years*

We are sheep with no shepherd
We are sheep with no straight and narrow
We are sheep with no meadow
We are sheep who take the dangerous pathway through
the mountain range
to get to the other side of the soul.
*from The Black Sheep*
KAREN FINLEY, *Shock Treatment*

Gently I enter this broken rectum of light,
a silver motorcycle on black wings.
SAPPHIRE

### directions to a poem

From Main Street:
It's best to leave well before dawn
Weather permitting, drive into the storm
Cross the bridge where the hemlock grows wild
These roots make the best medicine
Don't follow the tracks
Take the tunnel at the end of the light
Dig along fault lines
Press yourself between rocks and hard places
Wait for the undertow
When you think you're lost, you're there

JEWEL MATHIESON

## three of swords

Ground yourself, strip yourself down to blind, loving silence.

RUMI

for a few years in my late twenties I came as close as I have ever been to being a card-carrying psychic. While I didn't have a 900 number or a flashing pink neon palm in my window, I did do readings by appointment. This was a time of "dancing in the dark with strangers."

It all started at a weekend workshop on intuition. Twenty of us gathered in a big old house in Berkeley. All the shades were drawn, and we sat in the living room, in a circle, in the dark while the teacher talked us down into our bodies. She intoned primordial chants that transported us into a trance state where images floated to the surface of our minds. I had never before sat still for three days in the dark, and it had an overwhelming effect on me. It shifted my attention from my head to deep into my center, where I experienced the rumblings of my soul. It was like a three-day-long psychic flash opening me to everything. The world had no boundaries. I could feel the vibes of the guy next to me as if they were my own.

Not realizing how profoundly I had shifted, I returned home to Big Sur. The first sign that all was not normal was when, walking along, I couldn't feel my feet. I could see them, but they were very far away. It was a strange sensation floating down the hill with my skinny boyfriend chatting away beside me. He might as well have been speaking Farsi. His words were like beads in a rattle shaking around my head.

It was a true out-of-body experience. Completely disconnected from my body, I found myself zooming in and out of everybody else's. Boundaries were a thing of the past. I'd bump into someone on the path and start debating the merits of a clandestine affair they were having. Or sit down at lunch next to somebody and say, "Bummer, you got disinherited." Unfortunately, several people went into shock by peering into their deep dark secrets. Remember, it was the 1960s. For all they knew, an FBI informant was in their midst. To preserve all of our sanity, there had to be a way to ground this mysterious information. I chose to do Tarot readings. I had never used a Tarot deck before and actually could have done what I did without it, but it was strangely comforting to have something physical, something ancient, something visual between us.

During a reading for a middle-aged man from Ohio, he drew the three of swords—the image of a heart with three swords plunged through it. Immediately my own heart began beating furiously, and I felt sharp, intense pains in my chest, which doubled me over. I realized it wasn't my pain; it was his. His broken heart was beating in my body. Words poured out of me, describing his life in detail and all the events and relationships that had resulted in this incredible pain he was holding. As I spoke, my own body relaxed and my heartbeat eventually went back to normal.

It took nearly experiencing someone else's broken heart to shock me back into my own body. My heart had been cracked wide open into a level of intimacy that was beyond anything I had ever experienced. It was as if a veil had been lifted, showing me that if a boundary between ourselves and others existed at all, it was a filmy membrane at best. Once the membrane dissolves, we get to really know people beyond the biblical sense. We know everything they know even if they aren't aware that they know it. In fact, to my mind, a reading is when one person has decided to empower the other to tell them what deep down they already know. To read someone's mind you need to get out of the way, get over yourself and let what's going on in the other person flow through you. As my psychic sidekick Terry Iacuzzo says, it's like a blood transfusion.

Intimacy is the instinct of the heart. Whereas the ego would like us to believe and act as if we were separate little alien creatures who happen to share the same planet, the truth is that you and I are part of the same energy, connected on the most intimate level. Once we embrace the mystery of our own hearts we can effortlessly enter the dark of another heart because we are already there.

Basically, you can't fall in love with anyone else if you don't love yourself. Otherwise, who is doing the loving? Too often, people think that falling in love will make them whole. It's backwards. In the words of Sri Nisagadatta Maharaj, "Your love of others is the result of self knowledge, not its cause."

It takes a lot of effort to resist intimacy. Maintaining the illusion of our invulnerability keeps the ego busy 24/7. It has to come up with reasons not to connect to other people: she's too smart, I'll look bad, his checkbook is too light, she's too needy, he's too controlling, we're on different wavelengths. The excuses are endless. The moment we meet new people we begin the hunt for something to resist. We pass judgment on others for no reason except to bolster our defenses, to reinforce our armor, to hide ourselves behind an immovable mask.

On the dance floor, meeting complete strangers in the beat, you have the opportunity to rip off your mask and relax into the rhythm of connection. Sweat will melt your defenses away. Rhythms shatter one's need to judge, control, defend, push, blame. In the fleeting energy of the moment there is only the dance.

When you disappear in the dance, you lose all self-consciousness. You don't worry about how you look—if you're graceful or dumpy, fat or skinny, smiling or grimacing—all these superficial ego concerns dissolve. They're all illusions anyway. When you dance until there's nothing left but the dance, it is as if a door has been flung open; with one gentle push you fall into love, into the big, badass beat of the universe.

The irony is the deeper you look inside, the more tuned in you get to the bigger picture outside. You descend into your own depths, your own darkness. The intimacy of intuition is by nature dark. Not the paranoid, ego-driven darkness that has been passed down from generation to generation in superstitions designed to conjure up or protect us from fear, but the peaceful, soulful darkness of emptiness, the darkness of the Great Nothing from which we are all sprung.

How do we resolve the paradox of dissolving the boundaries that separate us from other people and maintaining a discrete, delightful self? One thing is clear, we need to keep one foot in each world—one in the physical world, one in the spiritual world. Both feet in one world doesn't work, because it either shuts us down or opens us up completely. The trouble is, we tend to divide the world that way, between "realists" and "dreamers," between standing in the physical world only, body-bound, anchored to material reality, and floating groundlessly in the spiritual world, mind-bound, unable to relate to the physical. Take a lesson from the birds who soar in the sky, sensing the earth's pull in every cell of their bodies and using the wisdom of both worlds to inspire their flight.

# raven

*When the heart weeps for what it has lost,*
*the spirt laughs for what it has found.*
SUFI APHORISM

Being mysterious is living theater. When we get over ourselves (having selves, that is) there are no roles to play, no lines
to memorize, no scenes to replay or dailies to watch. We are
free to improvise, to be authentic in every situation. There's no
more need to act. The footlights are off. We're in the dark; we
have to feel our way.

Where *are* our feelings? Are they in a safe-deposit box at
Chase Manhattan Bank? Unfortunately not; they're in the body,
and it is in the body that we can experience them and through
the body that we can express them. If we live in our heads all
the time, denigrating everything below the neck, it's only a matter of time before we will find ourselves on line at the phar-
macy with a prescription for Prozac. Repressing feelings is a
one-way ticket to depression and loneliness.

Loneliness is a phantom feeling. You're never alone once you've
made a connection to your mysterious, multifaceted, diamond,
glow-in-the-dark self.

Feelings are the language of the heart, but we have silenced
them. We talk about feelings, we think about feelings, but when
we actually feel them we get so scared we immediately shove

them back into the deepest chambers of our hearts. Yet none of us wants to be numb. We long to connect. We long to be real. We long to be intimate.

Intimacy is the transitory dissolution of boundaries, with animals, with trees, with flowers, with the groceries you bring home to feed your family. It happens with the minerals we mine from the earth and with the soil that provides our nourishment. It happens alone and it happens together, on airplanes, in bedrooms, on the dance floor, at a concert, a rally, a basketball game, even at the movies. It happens when we resonate on the same wavelength. Recently I saw *Monsoon Wedding*, a gorgeous film that, among other things, happens to be about romantic and familial intimacy. In one scene, a young man kneels inside an altar of candles set against a black sky holding a huge heart made of marigolds in front of his chest as an offering to his beloved, who, until that moment, has had no idea she was his beloved. In addition to the girl, he seduced every one of us in the audience. Had she rejected him there would've been an uprising in the Tower Theater in Sacramento on a Thursday afternoon.

Intimacy is a night-blooming flower. It thrives in the dark, the dark of the movie theater, the dark of the bedroom, the dark of the heart, the dark of the mouth. "When someone loves you, the way they say your name is different. You know that your name is safe in their mouth," says Billy, age four. Out of the mouths of babes . . .

Maybe our fear of intimacy is rooted in our fear of the dark, especially the deep dark within, the great unknown. We perceive our inner darkness as a void, an emptiness that fills us with anxiety. We try to stuff this black hole instead of realizing that we are the black hole and that its emptiness is actually a fathomless freedom.

Freedom can be a scary concept. What do we do when we let go of all expectations? Not just of ourselves but of others as well? How do we navigate in the black hole? We don't. We don't have to. Throw out your compass and disconnect your global positioning system. Let the dark do you. Trust that there is a big, old, wise, wondrous being within you that knows you intimately. Knows where you've been. Knows where you need to go. Even knows the unknowable things about you.

Intimacy is an open path, an etheric bridge between my consciousness and yours, my heart and yours. Crossing this bridge is thrilling if it makes us electric and alive. Why then do we so often get stuck at the toll booth? Because we don't want to pay the price: total surrender to vulnerability, spontaneity, and an open, unguarded heart. Intimacy requires us to risk all, to reveal all, including the big bad ego parts, the deep sensitive wounded parts, the everyday humdrum parts, and the fiery crazed creative parts. Everything. Every last bit.

Ravens fascinate me. They wear my favorite color, and they love unconditionally. Ravens mate for life, and if they're lucky they can spend about forty years together. Naturalists observing them have never witnessed tensions between raven mates. They are affectionate, honoring the bond they share till death, and when one dies the other mourns, often grievously, even dying of a broken heart. These dark beings have over twenty distinct songs of mourning, according to the officer in charge of them in the Tower of London. A friend mentioned the other day that there was a raven in her yard singing the strangest, saddest songs, day after day. And I thought, Of course! A brokenhearted raven would never try to think himself out of his pain or make a wall out of it. How vulnerable to sit in a tree and sing yourself inside out! As Shelley wrote, "I want to sing like birds sing, not worrying who hears or what they think."

Human beings may die of broken hearts in poetry, novels, and movies. But more often than not time and maybe a little therapy put an end to our grieving. No matter how intimate our relationships, we still consider the other person separate from us, and we most often hold part of ourselves back as a reserve—a reserve against betrayal, abandonment—a reserve that helps us deal with illness and death. It's the rational part of us looking out for number one. It's not necessarily a bad thing. You can't drop dead whenever somebody you love dies. Nevertheless, we can learn from the ravens what it looks like to totally surrender yourself to love and let it inspire and move you whenever and however it will.

"Intimacy is a difficult art," Virginia Woolf said, in one of the great understatements of the twentieth century. We seem to find infinite ways to block it from happening, though our bodies and our souls ache to flow over with it. Why not just give in and let yourself surrender? Falling in love takes practice. I'm not talking about serial relationships here. I'm talking about falling in love with love. So take your aching body over to the CD player and put on whatever music breaks through to your heart. Your heart is your body, and the dance is love. So let your body dance, and your heart will love. Dance your pain, dance your longing, dance your heart out. When there's nothing left to let go of, turn off the music, sit in the dark, and just listen to your heart beat.

## queenie

I have faith in nights.
RAINER MARIA RILKE

I used to ride a half-blind, jet-black Arabian mare named Queenie. A boy had shot out her right eye with a BB gun. She was my best friend, my first spiritual teacher, but I didn't know it at the time. She initiated me into the power of darkness and mystery. We used to ride every evening. We'd leave the road and cross the big empty field till we reached the railroad tracks. We'd wait for the evening train to barrel by so we could chase it across the field as twilight faded to black. She knew her way so well she didn't need eyes to see. We trusted ourselves to be taken by the wind.

That was long ago. Today I look back at the rides with

Queenie as a metaphor for intimacy. We never communicated with words, but I knew her and she knew me. Galloping through the dark, over fences, in and out of trees, she was my black beauty, my queen of the night. We were night-riders, me and Queenie. None of that daylight, bridle-path, horse-show shit for us.

I was born at night and never have been a day person. Something relaxes, awakens in me as twilight approaches. Night belongs to the moon. I do too. There's a whole different culture on the night shift. Those who sleep all day wake up at the edge of night; they dream in the daylight and daydream at night. Night people are like a Miles Davis solo; a different mood surrounds them, a different tempo.

Listen to the night. In the country or the city, it has a voice all its own, a mysterious, dark voice. In the city, sometimes a car radio breaks the spell. In the country, it's the crickets. And then you remember where you are—in the bosom of night.

The new moon holds
for one night long
the old moon in its arms.
BERTOLT BRECHT

How different the world looks under the influence of the moon with her shifting lights. Shadows disappear in the dark, but black shapes shift like old shamans as the moon transforms trees into giants, rocks into men. New worlds appear and disappear in the fluidity of her cool stare, unlike in the sunlight, where a tree is a tree and bush a bush. And all the while the moon keeps the backbeat of tidal rhythms.

Night is full of promise and night mares that move faster than the speed of light.

## raven down

How sweetly did they float upon the wings
Of silence, through the empty-vaulted night,
At every fall smoothing the raven down
Of darkness till it smiled!
JOHN MILTON

My friend Marty is blind. He lives in perpetual night. He brings a small carpet to my workshops and dances on it. I call it Marty's magic carpet. Anybody who wants to dance with him can join him and find a way to let him know they are there. The other dancers don't always see that he is blind, and people sometimes mindlessly crisscross his rug as if it weren't there. Funny, having 20/20 vision doesn't guarantee sight.

Dancing with a blind person throws us, takes us off guard. How will he know I have on my friendly face or that I am doing my best moves or that I need his approval or that I expect him to lead? How will he know the not-so-subtle messages that shoot off our bodies? He won't! For him touching is seeing. His darkness invites a more intimate connection. Marty belongs to the moon.

My son, Jonathan, moves onto the rug, gently leans into Marty's left shoulder, sinks down into his groove. They undulate together, like two dolphins crossing the great water, signaling each other's moves with sonar, comfortable with the darkness. Like the perpetual night at the bottom of the ocean, never rising to the surface or the light, Marty's dance is in a dark dream time. Jonathan borrows Marty's wisdom of darkness, a stranger escorted through depths his 20/20 eyes would otherwise never know. As the drums intensify, two men on a rug in the dark feel their way through the unknown and unpredictable into each other's hearts.

Years ago, another blind man danced with us. People avoided him as well, wouldn't risk the journey into a world so different from their own, couldn't move past their own fear of the big "D"—disability—wouldn't dream of entering a space so strange as that! So I blindfolded all of us for an hour and turned up the music. Their bodies were suddenly tense with fear. Dancing in the dark. Groping. For a moment they glimpsed what it might be like in a blind world, navigating the subways and busy streets of Manhattan or drifting in the country where silence gives few clues to orient oneself. After a short while, trusting their feet, they learned the magic of darkness, the tricks of negotiating what their eyes couldn't see.

Another way to experience the insights of darkness is to

have a blackout. Turn off your life for three days and three nights or however long you can without alienating your posse. No music, no TV, no phone, fax, or computer, no books, no writing, no to-do lists. Pull the blinds, cover the mirrors, and just be with yourself. Feel the rhythm of your life without anything to do—the undercurrents, what goes on beneath all that activity. Don't even cook meals—be simple and restrict your diet to water, juice, nuts, and fruit.

Darkness can be dangerous but also intriguing. In some cultures, darkness is simply the unknown, the mystery, nothing more, nothing less, and people venture into it expecting wonders. It's the tunnel into the holy unknown, an adventure into the unseen.

Once we connect intimately with the darkness inside ourselves, it will connect us to everything and everyone around us. Once we know the darkness, every moment can be a meditation. Meditation is the dark heart of prayer, the little black dress of the divine mother. And as my mother always said, "You can't get by without a little black dress." Meditation also transports us to the realm of intimacy where it is absolutely required to be real and to see the real in others. It is a gateway to compassion, the highest vibration of love.

# the dark light of the soul

> Ever since the beginning these twins are sewing. One sews with
> light and one sews with dark. . . . Each trying to set one more bead
> into the pattern than her sister, each trying to upset the balance of
> the world.
> LOUISE ERDRICH, *The Antelope Wife*

A black-box theater is ideal for my experimental theater workshops, where the point is to dive into the dark of our psyches
for characters. It creates the perfect mood. My favorite is the
Theater Artaud in San Francisco, named after the most anarchistic and shamanic force in modern theater. Antonin Artaud
ranted and raved as he searched for "true theater." He lamented
that "it has lost the feeling on the one hand for seriousness and
on the other for laughter; because it has broken away from
gravity, from effects that are immediate and painful—in a
word, from Danger."

Artaud and his rebellion against a theater of talking heads
intrigues me. Standing in his namesake theater with a group of
students last year, his spirit bounced off the black walls, in-
spiring my own search for true theater, a living art form that
heals our many splits and spiritually recharges us.

Artaud called the actor "an athlete of the heart," fearlessly
seeking to be real, to be raw, to affirm the marvel of emotions.
Actors, like athletes, have to prepare, work out, immerse themselves in their hearts, no longer standing outside themselves.

Artaud's athlete of the heart is the superhero of today. We all know what a burden it is to live in a culture whose heart is frozen. Today it's a survival art to reclaim our right to the full-bodied expression of our hearts. And this was what I was doing one Saturday afternoon in San Francisco with my motley crew of explorers.

From my perch on the edge of the elevated platform, I surveyed the room, now full of people dancing to the warmup music. It hurt to watch them, to be reminded of the fears that rob the human heart. Holding my breath, sinking into my own vulnerability, I touched a place of tenderness that threatened to make me weep. Their bodies, fearing emotional truths they were holding inside, moved cautiously around the room, like prisoners in exercise yards, searching for escape routes into joy, into freedom, beyond their broken hearts. As Robbie Robertson's *Unbound* pulsed, I pondered the source of all this emotional dysfunction and opened my mouth to say, "Okay, this is where we're at, so let's get specific about the negative energies that populate the dark side of the heart." But something stopped me before the words got out. Why did I automatically separate light and dark into good and bad? The duality was so ingrained in my subconscious it was part of my mindless speech.

When we equate dark with evil, we fall into a two-thousand-year-old trap, one that says bad guys always wear black, that black cats are bad luck, that blondes have more fun; one in which dark is considered negative, scary, dysfunctional. Every day, I hear myself or someone else perpetuate that legacy. But true darkness is distinct from the shadow world, where we shove all the stuff that we'd like to hide and that then stalks us. Darkness is our sanctuary, a place where we find our divinity. We should seek the darkness, not run from it.

Why must we see the world in Manichean terms—light versus dark, good versus evil? I never wanted to be Glinda the Good Witch, nor did I want to be the Wicked Witch of the West. I wanted to be the Witch of Contradictions, with dark hair and ruby slippers, but living just about anywhere but Kansas. I wanted to have skin whose color I could change at will, depending on where you stood with me, and you'd never know exactly where you stood. (If I was going to be a witch I was going to be a witch!) Come to think of it, Glinda was probably a fake blonde anyway.

Of course, it's tough to shake off a lifetime of conditioning. An Italian student of mine was really struggling with dark being anything but evil. I asked her to close her eyes. "Is it dark in there?"

"Yes," she stated.

"Is it evil?" I whispered.

"No." Her voice faltered.

"Open your eyes." She blinked. "Is it light?"

"Yes."

"Is everything you see good?"

"No."

What if, after we die, we discover that our souls are both light and dark? What do we do, send the dark part back? I guess that would mean that the light part of our soul is the part that gets to go shopping, ride in cabs, gab on the phone, lunch with friends, create religions, and oversee institutions of all sorts. The dark part? Well, maybe it could grow up to be a philosopher, a down-and-out artist, a punk rocker, or an undertaker.

So if our souls have two aspects, what do we know of the dark part? Maybe the dark represents the internal and eternal soul, what gives us common ground as human beings. Maybe it's the source we plug into when we meditate, in those moments when we feel our individual selves dissolving in the ocean of the universal being. Have we become unplugged from this energy source, the divine darkness within us? And is this why we frantically seek a charge from the outer world, the world of bright lights and big cities?

Is there no other way to look at the light and the dark? Well, a few billion people in the East, for a few thousand years, have found wholeness and harmony by embracing the dark feminine and light masculine that is in all and everything. Think yin and yang. And shamans, some fifty thousand years ago, sought out the darkness and stillness of caves to connect with the spirit of the Cosmic Mother.

The problem is that when the part of us in the light is not rooted in the dark, we end up cowering in the shadows, the realm of the ego. Ever the manipulator, the ego must create dualities and separations so it can assert its power by playing one side against the other. The old divide-and-conquer strategy.

In the light we can see our shadows and hide from them, if we must. In the dark our shadows are hidden from us, threatening to leap out, to call our bluff, to expose our secrets, fears and doubts. The trick is to meet our shady ego characters in the darkness and dance them into the light. Like Kali, you devour your shadows in your dance, where they nurture and energize you. On the dance floor, you can work your ego out, transforming boredom into a tossing, turning, restless dance. Or letting anger take on its amazing multidimensional moods, carrying you from resentment through rage through numbness. Getting to know all these shadowy aspects frees your raw energy to move.

And then there are days when you can't get to the dance floor and the shadow-monster ego-mob-boss attacks your head and takes control of your mouth, your phone, your car, your entire psyche. It's like the main character in Banana Yoshimoto's novel *Amarita* says: "The me that's only me is the only me I can't remember."

That true, soulful me will always be in the dark. That's why we need to free ourselves from the didactic model where light is good and dark is evil, for it cuts us off from the mystery of our inner and unseen world, a world that is much vaster than the seen world. A cut flower only lasts a week at most, but a flower attached to its roots can be reborn season after season. When it's connected to the dark within, its very nature is to seek the light. To be cut off from one's inner source, what Dylan Thomas calls "the force that through one green fuse drives the flower," leaves us afraid to close our eyes, sit in the dark, listen to the silence, savor the emptiness, fall into the lap of the

Cosmic Mother. Saddest of all, it prevents us from appreciating the holiness of each other.

So how do we dissolve the artificial dualities of the ego? For me there are only two ways—movement or stillness. Not movement full of steps or stillness full of thoughts, but feeling the movement in the stillness and the stillness in all motion. We need to quiet our demons by dancing them until they are set to rest. Or meditate until the bastards jump ship. Really be still or really move. Whichever you do, do it mindfully.

When you dance in the dark, you'll discover that all dimensions—light and dark, ego and soul, stress and serenity, petulance and placidness, cacophony and calm—exist simultaneously as part of the universal energy that infuses all things. Weave them all into your moving meditation.

I used to love to sit in the dark beside my sleeping child, to rest my hand lightly on his back and feel his tiny shape expanding and contracting with each breath till I was breathing in sync with him. Often I nursed him in the dark, unable to see him. Feeling him melt into me, sucking my breast, twirling my nipples with his tiny fingers, I'd surrender to this dark, sensuous, nurturing place within me, a place I never would have found without him.

We can all reclaim the innocence of darkness for ourselves. Once you do, your fear will be transformed into fascination. As children we happily coexisted in the vast, empty, unclaimed space where darkness and light intermingled. As adults, we feel compelled to fill up and overschedule our lives, no longer seeing either the light or the dark because we are mired in the shadows. But they're both there, just beneath the surface, unified like some giant exotic fish who ogles us curiously. It takes courage to dive down under, look that fish in the eye, and let it carry us deeper into the mystery.

> Lord, You have plunged me into the bottom of the pit,
> into the black depths of the abyss.
> Your terrors have reduced me to silence,
> and my only friend is darkness.
> PSALM 88

> You [God] see in the dark
> because daylight and dark
> are all the same to you.
> PSALM 139

# if you don't wear black,
# don't call me back

> I bring my small corrections to the world, but they stem from what I am and what I am is my taste.
> BORIS GREBENSHIKOV

For me, infinite equals black. Black is forever and then some; it will outlast light. Black is the beginning, the source, the before and the after, the Alpha and the Omega. We'll all be sucked into a black hole one of these days, so we may as well hang with it.

One spring, I found myself sitting in a favorite black dress next to a very sophisticated nine-year-old in the back seat of a silver Mercedes cruising uptown to the ballet. "How come you always look like you're going to a funeral?" my little friend asked.

"Gee," I told her, "I guess I represent the void."

She rolled her eyes.

I said, "Okay, actually, this medicine man, Hyemeyohsts Storm, once told me to always wear black, that black is my power color. Deep down I'd always known that. I'd been wearing black all my life, except for this brief purple phase because a psychic told me I was hiding in black."

My companion seemed unimpressed.

"Something about black comforts me," I told her.

As we drove through the streets of Manhattan, images of black flashed through my mind, mingling with neon, flashing taillights, and the glare of approaching headlights. I grew up with Black Beauty and Black Power, and grew down with Black Sabbath and the Black Crowes. Later, shamans taught me that black is the color of the west on the medicine wheel, the direction linked to the earth, the female body, introspection, change, death, and intuition. Sitting at the eastern quadrant of the wheel, my favorite place to sit, I faced the west and darkness, racing into it as if transported by invisible forces into the dark unknown.

Nine-year-olds on their way to the ballet do not care about the unknown.

As we cruised up Broadway, Daniella explained to me how she spent her fourth year on this planet exclusively in black. What happened was she fell in love with the Pirates of the Caribbean ride at Disney World and wouldn't leave the state of Florida without a black leather skull vest. Before long she wore it every day with black leggings, a black T-shirt, and black baby biker boots. She became obsessed with Batman and begged to have her pink room painted black. In her opinion pink had a curse—whenever you touched pink you started to spill things and you had to touch black immediately to break the spell. I told her how I once wore pink to a session I was teaching and one of my students said she couldn't learn from me in pink.

"See?" she said.

"Okay, Miss I-haven't-even-made-it-to-double-digit-hood, why is black still your favorite color?"

"Black makes grownups look all depressed and spiritual, like they're going through a hard time. But I look good in black because I haven't lived long enough to go through that much."

Just then we entered the parking garage. She turned to me and said, "Anyway, everybody has black pupils so we all see the world through black."

I see the world through the iridescent black of a raven's wing, the sleek black of a panther's skin, the luxurious black of silk velvet, the tough black of smooth leather, the ethereal black of soot, the shiny black of a limousine, the all-enveloping black of a nun's habit, the thick black of Japanese hair, the ominous black of a thundercloud, the echo of the black cry, the mysterious pull of the black continent within.

There are Native Americans who teach of ten chakras. My favorite is the ninth, a black sphere located between the feet. Inside this beautiful black luminous egg is your medicine, your destiny, the way you are meant to serve. So how do you crack open the ego and release the mystery? You dance and ask with all your devotion to be shown the way.

## dancing in the dark

The unknown is the last thrill ride.
TERRY IACUZZO

A friend once sent me a news clipping about a lady in Layton, Utah, who survived being stranded overnight on an icy, snow-covered mountain. How did she manage this miracle? She reached into her own darkness, found all the songs stored in her, and replayed them to inspire her dance. She didn't sit down in the snow and say, "There's no jukebox so I think I'll lay down and die." She danced all night in the freezing cold pitch-black darkness and kept herself alive.

Dancing in the dark fuels our inner heat.

## black is where it's at

A billion stars go spinning through the night,
blazing high above your head.
But in you is the Presence that will be,
when all the stars are dead.
RAINER MARIA RILKE

Although the spot on my lung remains a mystery, surgery itself was a descent into the dark place where I confronted not only the possibility of my death but my relationship to the unknown. How would I receive the black-hooded Grim Reaper? Should I devour garlic every night, as Mel Brooks recommended as the two-thousand-year-old man? Could I go gracefully? Would there really be a tunnel of light? Those questions slipped quickly through my mind, leaving me to ponder something Allen Ginsberg once said: "Buddha died and left behind this great big emptiness."

Death is the ultimate dissolution of boundaries. Our bodies merge with the earth, and our souls are liberated to soar in the spirit. At birth the universe breathes us out into our bodies, and at death it sucks us back into its big belly, perhaps to be born again. Who knows?

Death is where we lose the light and become pure darkness. In life, we each have our own personal truths that change from moment to moment; it's totally relative. I'm tired, I'm hungry, I'm hot, I'm cold, I really want that black cashmere cape. But underneath rumbles the big truth, an eternal truth that is independent of our whims and fantasies, desires and moods. When we die, the light of the little truth goes out, and we are left in the consummate intimacy of the dance.

During my stint in Big Sur, I was having a conversation in a parking lot with a young doctor who served the community. My eyes were riveted by his headband, and as I looked at it, it gave me shivers. It was a Friday, and we made dinner plans for Monday. The moment he left, I went and sat in my car and sobbed for no apparent reason. Sunday afternoon, during tea at a Big Sur hot spot, a local came screaming into the restaurant. A car had just gone over the cliff by Gorda Mountain. I froze. "Was it a doctor, by any chance?" I asked. "Yeah, it was the Esalen doctor." He didn't die right away, but spent the next few weeks in a coma with severe head injuries. Every night, I visited him and prayed for his recovery, even though I'd already seen his ghost dancing in the parking lot. There are so many levels of intimacy, so many ways to hold each other, to touch each other in the dark.

The ego wants to keep you locked in the light, in denial of

the dark. Obsessed with your personal truth and afraid of surrendering to the bigger truth that we are all being danced by
the same divine dervish. We fear the dark and death because the
ego has demonized them and prevented us from exploring their
depths. The ego always wants to swim in the shallow end of the
pool. In truth, we need as much diving practice as we can get in
this lifetime so we're not afraid of the next. Death is just another dance, another dive.

An added bonus to making peace with the dark side before
you kick the bucket is that you can access eternal wisdom in
this lifetime. The Native American teacher Sun Bear often told
the story about a spirit guide who was his source of intuitive
wisdom. The guide was an *ancient one,* meaning that he'd been
dead for about 150 years, and his advice was always deep, wise,
and steeped in tradition. But every time Sun Bear followed this
guide's advice, it got him in trouble. Bewildered by all this, Sun
Bear sought out his earthly mentor, one of the elders of the
tribe, whose judgment he trusted above all others. He laid out
all his woes about his spirit guide as the elder gazed at the
ground, listening patiently. Sun Bear finished his list of com-
plaints, then waited for his companion's words of wisdom to
bring some clarity to the whole sad story. After several moments
of silence, the elder looked up and announced, "Dead don't
make you wise!"

Gazing up into the night sky, infinity is darker than dark.
Endless space is our only container, infinity is our only boundary. For a moment I focus not on the stars, not on heavenly

bodies, not even on black holes, but on space, pure space, the emptiness that has no beginning, middle, or end, where form explodes out of nothingness, where big bangs are commonplace and filled with mystery, where getting born again and again is a simple enough matter, no need for holy water or raving evangelists.

There was a time, not so long ago, when astronomy was about what we could see in the sky, about lights moving in recurring patterns and the glow of star systems and comets. But all that has changed. Now it's about what we cannot see. Astronomers are facing the fact that stars and galaxies, and all that inhabits them, are but tiny specks in a churning sea of dark matter. As Rebecca Goldstein brilliantly put it in her novel *Properties of Light*, "I figured darkness to be not the absence of light, but rather light the absence of darkness."

According to recent news, our latest space probe is being pulled way off its trajectory by some force that we do not quite understand. The only explanation is that there is a large physical body that we cannot see and its gravitational pull is causing it to shift. We now know that our universe is over 90 percent dark matter, a vast area that is invisible to us, in which it is quite possible that there is a parallel universe that lies perhaps no more than a few millimeters away from our own. Ask a high school physics teacher about this and he will probably laugh at you, but ask a theoretical physicist and she will nod in full agreement. Moreover, we know that there are black holes and wormholes and the possibility of stable rings within these holes where we might be transported between universes instantly, with no need for a spaceship.

What was once only a science fiction fantasy is now the emerging reality. Meanwhile, in metaphysics, black is a state of mind that can take you anywhere you want. A little attitude adjustment is all you need to allow the veils to drop and the masks to shatter so you can stop everything, sit in the dark of your own heart, and honor your longing to connect to the source of your existence.

> I mean, no candlelight, no firelight, not one lumen
> This is definitely the dark we're dancing in,
> As we ponder the meaning of our existence here—
> Let me ask the equally imponderable question:
> Where is here?
> Of course we are lucky to have something under our feet
> On which to do our dancing.
> That's something.
> E. L. DOCTOROW, *City of God*

# slow dancing with chaos

The thing about death, though,
is that it eliminates so many
options.

TOM ROBBINS, *Fierce Invalids Home from Hot Climates*

why does the wind
blow me so wild?
it is because i'm
nobody's child

PATTI SMITH, *Rock n Roll Madonna*

There is, one who knows not what sweet mystery about this sea,
whose gently awful stirrings seem to speak of some hidden soul
beneath.

HERMAN MELVILLE, *Moby-Dick*

## silver desert dj's

They give us the beat
A rolling rhythm that rocks us back into our center
home of the hieroglyphic dance
choreographed from cave drawings
exhumed from bellies
They give us the beat
A heart beat marking time for the journey home
Fused palms part as drum sermons crack through bones
They give us the beat
The wild beat that unhinges thighs at broken angles
begging to be set right again in the beat
into the beat of angel's wings
Joy is the line they cast
where fish leap from pore to pore
They give us the beat
driving us to rest in stillness
where earth and heaven sigh
to lie with ancestors after one last dance
the oracle being poured into our exhale
They give us the beat, the lost language
They take us to where fevered feet etch scriptures
in the deep end of the floor

JEWEL MATHIESON

all shook up

What sticks to memory, often, are those odd little fragments that have no beginning and no end.
TIM O'BRIEN, *The Things They Carried*

**O**nce I did a reading for a grand dame of New Orleans so-
ciety. She lived in an exquisite rambling Victorian mansion surrounded by lush gardens. We sat in her sitting room off the
parlor, a cloistered little womb room insulated with dark wood
paneling, the air heavy with the scent of magnolias. This was at
a time in my intuitive evolution when I was training myself to
pick up information only when I wanted to, not just because
someone happened to be seated next to me on a bus or at a dinner. So my clients were asked to bring a personal object to help
me tune into their energy, something precious that they'd had
for a while and preferably something they had worn.

My southern belle handed me an elaborately set emerald ring. As my hand closed around it, images flooded my mind— elephants, a piece of brilliantly embroidered red cloth, a polo field, a silver tea service—but she rejected every suggestion as having nothing to do with her. This had never happened to me before, so I kept reeling off images. Nothing seemed to relate to her life. My inner world began to spin out. Finally, in exasperation, I asked her where she had gotten the ring. "My grandmother bought it at an estate auction in India," she replied. As soon as she said "India," it clicked. I was picking up the vibes of the original owner. The ring was so charged with her energy, her vitality, her sense of her inner and outer worlds, that the two subsequent owners had failed to make an impression on it. It's amazing that the mind is so powerful it can imprint an object.

Readings have taught me to slow dance with chaos, even when it's coming at me from the outside. Last December, I choreographed a performance piece for a new Manhattan club. During dress rehearsal, I fell off the stage onto my head, resulting in a major concussion. The biggest blizzard of the century hit on opening night. I entered the club at 11:23 p.m., and what to my wondering eyes should appear but 200 totally drunk people dressed as Santas lurching around on the dance floor. This is our audience? It must be a David Lynch movie. The fire alarm went off during our first number, and ten firement in gear began weaving their way through the drunk Santas. I remembered something that avant-garde choreographer

Merce Cunningham said, "Chaos is only chaos if you think of it as chaos." Okay. Deep breath. What's my intention here? The show must go on.

Chaos is bi-directional—it can happen inside, it can happen outside. For me the teaching is that there is a path through chaos and that path is my intention. I stayed clam and on track with the doyen even though a big part of me wanted to run out the door. It also definitely occured to me to flee the club, but I stayed true to my intention to direct the show in spite of a major concussion, blizzard, 200 drunk Santas and deejay who just had to sabotage my choregraphy by playing a Martin Luther King speech during our sexiest, hottest number.

Intention carries us through the hard times. Think of it as the intuition of the mind, a powerful, creative force that can not only imprint objects but actually influence world events. Was it coincidence that on 9/11/2002 the New York State Lottery numbers came up as 911?

The mind-field is chaotic, and it's possible to feel overwhelmed in this vortex of energy and imagery. But if we practice navigating it with the intention of a wizened old Native American tracker, we can open ourselves to clues, signs, and symbols in the wilderness that lead us to our quarry. Trackers need a mission, a vision to propel them through thick and thin, to ground them in the chaos of it all. The fast track to being a tracker is dancing.

Put on some gentle, rolling chaos music. Place your feet shoulder-width apart and plant them there. Gently bounce to the beat of the music without moving your feet too much or jumping off the floor. This will help you relax as you move the rest of your body. Soften your knees so they cushion your bounce. As you shake, relax your face, gently moving your head so that your neck feels supported. Next, bounce and shake your shoulders. Keep adding parts of your body—arms, hands, fingers, hips, knees, thighs, legs—without eliminating the ones you just jiggled and bounced. Take a minute or two for each body part to feel the external and internal shaking.

Keep going until your whole body is shaking as if gentle, rolling thunder is rumbling through you. When the music stops, feel the pulse of chaos that moves in you, even when your exterior appears quiet and serene. The Sufis shook for long periods of time to create a state of trance. So did the Shakers, the shaking Quakers.

When you practice shaking yourself up, you don't have to get thrown when the universe shakes you up.

## and the beat goes in

I am the primitive of the way I have discovered.
PAUL CEZANNE

Dancing chaos is the survival art of our time. You wake up on a sunny Tuesday morning, pour yourself a cup of coffee, turn on the news, and watch thousands of people die instantly in an inferno of terror. Or maybe you have your coffee in a café and a young girl walks in wearing a trench coat and blows herself up. Or a tank rolls down your street and leaves your home in rubble before you even have a chance to think about coffee. Expecting the unexpected has become our way of life.

A lot of people can't handle this and are racing for prescriptions to dull the throbbing in their heads. The problem is the head. When chaos gets trapped in the head, it has nowhere to go. It's like living in a panic room.

Trust me, the only way out is through your feet. When I was eleven years old, my dad almost died of cancer. All of a sudden, my idyllic childhood fell to pieces. Being the oldest child, I took it upon myself to try to hold it all together; not just hold myself together but my parents and siblings as well. It was like trying to control a forest fire. As soon as I got one feeling under control, another would flare up. Terrified of the emotional chaos that was brewing inside of me, I did everything in my power to deny it.

Flash-forward ten years, two continents, and twenty-seven boyfriends. I am a dancer now, struggling to mold my body into the shapes created by Martha Graham, José Limón, and God knows how many other dance gurus. The more I try to control the chaos inside me by controlling my body, the more I end up in the chaos of my head. Liberation comes when I find my feet—not Martha's or José's feet.

Big Sur is a womb of rhythm. On a sweet day, I'd relax to the pounding surf, the strumming of the wind through the trees, the occasional crescendo of a falling rock. On another day, I'd tremble by the window watching boulders fly through the air, waves crash against the cliffs, trees whipping, breaking, and cracking. And then the silence, the stillness as if it were all a dream. Big Sur was chaos, a perfect mirror for my inner landscape. A perfect place to let it all escape. A perfect place to get out of my head and into my body.

Primed for release, all it took was five cowboys with conga drums to catalyze my flight. Dancing to the ancient beat passed down through generations of hands on skin, I found a way to break in, to break out, to break through. The chaos that had been bubbling inside me like a volcano threatening to erupt began to flow out through my dance and ignite my soul. As my head let go and my feet kicked in, my heart opened and poured itself into the dance.

There was no turning back. There was only surrender. Surrender to the rhythm of chaos—a process of going inside, connecting with the flow of my energy, finding its edge, and leaping off of that edge.

All the losses, the fears, the heartbreaks, and traumas—each and every one of them became its own dance, and this form of dancing became my prayer and my practice, a way to transform suffering into art.

When we let our panic dance, it doesn't change the situation, just our way of dealing with it. Without chaos in your head, your mind can move more freely and follow its intuitive radar. So when your world crashes, don't sit paralyzed in your living room, in shock or denial. Feel your feelings, let them move through you, find the dance that rocks you to your roots.

Hidden in the chaos, like the eye of the hurricane, is the moving center, your power center, a place deep in your belly, three fingers below the navel, where all the good stuff is waiting to be felt. It is in the moving center where all polarities converge; light and dark, good and evil, male and female, elephant and mouse. It's a place of perfect equilibrium and harmony. If only we could resist the temptation to choose one side or the other, we would be here more often. It's the only place where we can sit back and be fascinated by the chaos of our inner and outer worlds, instead of getting all stressed out about it. In the *Bhagavad Gita,* Krishna counsels the warrior Arjuna to be still, to be at perfect peace even in the chaos of battle.

The teaching of chaos is to constantly seek the opposite and accept the contradictions. When you're feeling joy, tune into your sorrow. When you're feeling writer's block, keep your hand moving on the page. When you're feeling rushed, move more slowly. When you're paralyzed with fear, crank up the volume and dance.

# in the groove

The journey of the meditation is downward, towards the roots.
OSHO

Sitting on my couch in Manhattan on a freezing January morning, it hit me that there was going to be an earthquake in Big Sur in April during the week I was scheduled to be teaching at Esalen. My husband Rob immediately counseled me to call and cancel. I did call and eventually revealed my reasons for backing out—one, there was going to be an earthquake, and two, I was going to be trapped, neither of which are things I would sign up for. They weren't too happy and probably thought that living on the East Coast had pushed me over the edge. Finally someone on the other end of the line convinced me to come. The north road had been cut off for weeks, and they were hurting financially.

Come April, I flew out with Rob and a bunch of musicians. The north road was still closed, so we circled around the southern route. Just as we crossed a particularly treacherous stretch, we heard a rumble, and a huge landslide cut off the road immediately behind us. Trapped! One of the musicians from the car behind us crossed the slide on foot; the other sped back to L.A.

The workshop started on Sunday evening, and during my introduction these words rolled off my tongue: "I know we are meant to end Friday at noon, but the workshop will end Thursday at four." Somebody asked me why. Who knew? Nobody was more surprised by my pronouncement than me.

On Tuesday afternoon, we were all dancing *chaos,* so involved in our own seismic activities that we didn't even realize a quake had happened until we left the room and saw all these pale, freaked-out people hanging onto the Esalen deck for dear life. Both of my premonitions had come true. Home free! By Thursday, my vibe had relaxed, the workshop had gelled, and I started questioning my decision to leave that day at 4:00. However, my keyboard player, already unnerved by events, simply picked up his synthesizer and headed for the door. So we left.

At 4:00 p.m. exactly, the southern road opened, and we breezed through. At 4:20 there was another landslide and the road closed, trapping everyone at Esalen for the next few days. The musicians in the back seat were looking a bit pale and freaked out at this point. They still couldn't wrap their heads around this whole chain of events. Neither could I. Heads don't work in these situations.

Like my musicians, most people don't enjoy earthquakes, mental or physical. It's called low chaos tolerance. Even prefer to living in quiet suburbs and driving big, safe cars doesn't help. Chaos finds us. Arguments with lovers, moments of great indecision when nothing makes sense, getting lost in a strange city, all these experiences transport us to the chaos zone. From the time we're born, we're taught to control our impulses, live by the rules, and get our act together. Stay on track. Falling apart is not encouraged. And surely, nobody in their right mind would want to sky-dive out of their own sense of order and free-fall into the mysterious order that exists at the center of chaos. The irony is that most of us think that if we let go of control, our lives will spin out of control, when letting go of control is the only way to keep our lives within control.

Robert, Jonathan, and I went upstate to do a workshop with a Native American elder. The group gathered on Friday for our introduction. Grandfather Whistling Elk concluded the evening by saying, "Tomorrow morning there'll be a sweat." He turned to go. Hands shot up. "What time?" "Where?" "What do we bring?" Over his shoulder, he responded, "You'll know." "How will we know?" "Ask a tree," he said and left the room.

The room dissolved in total confusion, with all of its brides-maids—insecurity, anger, and frustration—but there was nothing to do but go to bed and trust in the universe that we would know. And we did. The sweat started at 11:20, and everyone was on the spot.

According to Webster, *chaos* is either "confusion" or "an immeasurable emptiness." Thanks, Noah—real helpful. Well, actually, he was on to something. For me, it's both, depending on whether I'm resisting it or in its flow. Resisting it, trying to control it, imposing our will upon it, or hammering it into an order we're more familiar with, an order where we think we know what's going to happen next, is a recipe for self- or otherwise destruction. Left to its own devices, chaos is simply an energy, a natural phenomenon like an earthquake. It's futile to try to control it, yet we persist in driving ourselves crazy doing just that. One guy stayed up all night worrying about missing the sweat lodge. Five minutes in, he passed out from sheer exhaustion and had to be taken out.

Burdened by our ego, our shadow partner, we move like tired, thirsty old toads on a salt-parched desert. It weighs us down. Our ego prevents us from surrendering to the flow of chaos, from trusting our intuition and using it imaginatively. It wants us numb and anesthetized. Basically, the ego is a necrophiliac.

Best to surf waves of energy—be they grief or joy, anxiety or ecstasy, confusion or clarity. The trick is to remain empty and not hold onto energy. If you hold on, you wipe out. If you let go, the energy can transport you to the stillpoint, a place of immeasurable emptiness, of infinite potential.

We are in a chaos cycle now, all of us, the whole world. In the beginning there was the Great Mama who nurtured us in her womb. Life was cycles and rituals and shamans and druids and dreamers. We were part of her flow, and she was part of our dance. Then came Papa-Son with his lines and boundaries, hierarchies and authorities. This was the era of kings and popes and armies and fortifications—Great Walls and Iron Curtains. All the clear rules of childhood. But childhood doesn't last forever, even for a civilization. Hormones kick in and puberty kicks butt and walls come tumbling down. The Cold War is over, to be replaced by anarchistic terrorism. Gender is up for grabs, and religion is down for the count. Even the weather is defying prediction.

To survive the chaos of the outer world, we have to trust the chaos of our inner world. We have to trust the seemingly bizarre pronouncements of our intuition, even if it tells us to pick up and leave a successful workshop before it is finished, or back out of what appears to be a gold-plated contract, or hire someone whose resume is weak but whose presence is strong.

Chaos is the world beat, and it's essential to know how to move inside and through it and let it move inside and through us. Chaos is the beginning and the end, where everything springs up and everything lies down. I'm not talking about pandemonium here, like those high school days when substitute teachers showed up. I'm talking about cosmological chaos, out of which bursts truths way beyond human ingenuity or ego. It's where science dances with metaphysics and where Fractal Man, the newest superhero from the astrophysics realm, steps in. "Relax, baby!" he croons. "Consider the possibility that what you perceive as disorder is just another piece of a higher order you can't yet grok and maybe never will."

Fractals are a big deal these days. Physicists tell us they are the unique, seemingly random patterns that occur in the midst of the chaos, patterns like veins in leaves, veins in our hands, lines in our faces, and patterns of cracks across the earth, recording the unpredictable movements of events too complex to plot. We're put together the same way. My favorite computer engineer, Homer Smith, said, "If you like fractals, it is because you are made of them. If you can't stand fractals, it's because you can't stand yourself. It happens."

Ask yourself why, of the perhaps tens of millions of sperms and dozens of eggs produced by your parents, that particular mama egg and that particular papa sperm came together to produce the being that you are today. Come to think of it, what makes the lines in your hands, the swirls of your finger-prints different from mine? We're all fractals and that is the sheer imaginative genius of chaos.

Just as fractals are the hidden order in chaos, the stillpoint is the hidden intelligence in the swirl of our lives, the hidden truth in our body. It's the polestar that guides us through this rhythm of letting go. After we've dumped everything we don't need back into the dance—worries, stress, tension, resentment, fear, insecurity, everything we don't need—there's nothing left of us but a naked soul, the part of us that not only seeks empti-ness; but is made of it. Chaos is the way to emptiness; the way to emptiness is to empty—to let go.

# losing the groove

Nothing happens until something moves.
ALBERT EINSTEIN

A buzz saw jars me awake. This can't be happening, I tell my-self. My loft is my womb, my sanctuary, and it's been taken over by Hammer Man and Saw Man and Drill Through the Ceiling Lady. They're renovating the loft above mine. Drills, hammers, power saws. Deconstructing, reconstructing, it's all noise to me. Outside a guy drills a hole in the street. The phone rings five times before the machine kicks in. My life is being violated. Tea is my saviour. Unfortunately I have to get up to make it. My cir-cuits are overwrought, my senses warped. Last night a huge rat ran across the dairy isle in the health food store while I silently screamed, "Is nothing sacred?" A siren. The beat of our times is brutal.

The only appropriate response is to drown out one brutal beat with another, so I put on Bob Holyroyd's "Drumming Up a Storm" and do my impersonation of a jackhammer. Eventu-ally, there's nothing left but rhythm.

When faced with adversity, we have two choices—resistance or acceptance. While it might be tempting to pack up and move to Kauai, last time I was there they had a Class 5 hurri-cane. Better to dance in place and trust the dance to move you.

# chaos blues

Thou hast turned for me my mouring into dancing.
PSALM 30:11

Chaos is letting go—letting go of people when they die, relationships when they fall apart, emotions when they threaten to destroy us, thoughts when they sabotage us, memories when they prevent us from moving forward. Each of us will be tested ten thousand times in one lifetime.

It's part of the human drama to form attachments, and it's part of the chaotic nature of reality to shake and break those attachments. When they break, we feel sorrow. The healthy response is to surrender and let the grief move you and move through you. Cry and get on with it. The unhealthy response is to either tough it out, deny it, or wallow in it—a direct route to the analyst's couch.

Loss requires grieving, and grieving requires shattering, and shattering is letting go into chaos. The opposite, resistance to chaos, happens when we dissociate from our hearts, our losses, for it is then that we dissociate from our humanness, separate ourselves from our part in the broader drama of life. If parents lose a child, whether through an accidental drowning or a suicide bombing, they experience the shock and grief of all parents everywhere.

If you don't surrender to chaos then you become something rigid in a universe that is moving. Out of reality, out of nature, out of it. Just as you end up paralyzed by depression if you don't surrender to sadness. The deepest teaching of chaos is the experience of surrender. Chaos allows nothing less.

My friend died suddenly of an aneurysm. The family was in shock. I was in shock. She was the mother of my three step-sons. They were shattered. Surely this was a time when chaos gave us little chance to catch up. At the cemetery, the three young men in black suits each shoveled dirt onto their mother's coffin three times before passing the shovel on to those who were willing. The first shovelful dropped with a thunderous thud; our hearts trembled in its finality. And as the dirt con-tinued to fall, I held one of my sons, both of us sobbing.

She was buried on Mother's Day, and as her son eloquently pointed out in his eulogy, it was a cruel irony, in that she was all mother. That was her mission, her spiritual destiny in this lifetime. His speech was a brilliant catalyst for anyone who had a mother, had lost a mother, or was a mother. He touched us all, moved us deeply into a collective recognition of the power and presence of Mother.

Thank God for funerals, a societally sanctioned time to sur-render to chaos. You are expected to fall apart, and it's okay. Traditions like wakes, sitting shiva, building a pyre, or saying a mass all create safe space to mourn. Writing a eulogy gave my stepson an opportunity to channel his sorrow into an offering, a communion. Listening to his eulogy gave us an opportunity for cathartic release.

Rituals can be a port in the storm. So can maps. Even though it all looks like craziness and chaos, if you really pull back there's an order, a grand scheme of things. Mercifully, after hundreds and thousands of years, human societies have devised all kinds of imginative, creative ways—liturgies, rituals, maps—to guide us through these dark nights of the soul.

Sorrow is an important part of chaos. It's the energy of emotion, release, letting go. Think about somebody, anybody you know, and contemplate their losses. Maybe they lost their childhood or the use of some part of their body, or a job, or a relationship, or a dream. Life and loss go together like twisted sisters. Even in the breakdown of one's life there is an intelligence at work.

A timeless map helped me guide a friend through the wilderness of sorrow. She was depressed, full of regrets, falling apart at the seams. The doctors gave her Zoloft. It didn't do it for her. She moved beyond depression into despair, and that was where she was when we met for lunch. Her face quivered as she spoke. Her eyes were bleak. She had looked too long into a big black hole, and it had swallowed her. She ordered asparagus soup and pink lemonade. I had a veggie burger and contemplated our twenty-four years of dancing through it all together. *Nomad* pulsed in the background.

As my friend spoke her disillusionment, her regret resonated in me. We were in familiar territory. She was a falling star in a dark hole. I knew this place. You do, too.

Sometimes we really need structure, something to hang on to, a compass in the forest, radar in the storm, a beam of light in the darkness. Sometimes we think we're losing it totally, and we need to know others have passed through this space and lived to tell of it, that it's an organic, necessary part of our awakening. Maps don't just help us locate where we are but where we are coming from and where we might be going.

"Years ago I was doing Arica work," I told her. "The teacher, Ichazo, shared a Gurdjieff map that I've turned to many times for a sense of place and direction, for affirmation that nothing stands still and that our darkest moments can be the most profound."

Gurdjieff had mapped the journey we take from belief to samadhi, covering all the psychic territories in between. At the lowest, most basic level, the starting point on the map, we have a belief, an explanation for every possible situation, person, place, thing. We've got the whole thing tied up neatly with a bright blue ribbon. Remember Archie Bunker? He always had an answer, a neat or not-so-neat cubbyhole for everything under the sun.

From belief we shift to dogmas, where we seek our security in collective identities—religious, political, social, whatever works for us at that moment. But then we have a big bang and slide fully into self-importance. Now we are superstars in our own little universes. We make the rules, fall prey to our own hype. Nowhere left to go at this point but above it all.

Take a quick shuttle flight off to philosophy. Now we can just sit back and spin our theories like a mad violin spider.

Eventually—well, hopefully—we get tired of hearing only our own voices spinning around in our heads, and we slip unnoticed into disillusionment with everything, everyone, including our own brilliance. There seems nowhere left to go but into pure nihilism. Become a junkie, live in the streets, commit yourself to death one way or another.

This nihilistic, death-courting place is a relatively high level of consciousness, believe it or not. It's not a happy place, not a secure one, but definitely based on something real, even if we can't quite grasp it. Then, eventually, we come face to face with all that we regret. This is the bridge, a crossing of the great water, one step closer to our spiritual destiny.

Many tears later and we start the awesome task, the alchemical transformation of regret into wisdom. The gates open. Wisely, we stand at the threshold of the final spiritual frontier, dumping thousands of beliefs, dogmas, identities, spiraling inward to the Zen mind, the empty mind, even beyond chaos, to the dazzling brilliance hidden in the depths of the black hole, the darkness, where nothing reigns supreme. We now understand the task, to let go of thinking altogether. We've learned to be in the moment and find a practice that will help us stay there.

"There's no two ways about it. You are in regret," I tell my friend. "If it makes you feel any better, think of it as the last step before the bridge to nirvana." It's funny, but we can let go of the most profound sorrows—a dad who left, a lover who died, a pet who ran away—because we didn't create them, we are not responsible for them. Time heals those wounds, and sometimes a little therapy. But the ones that remain, the ones we can't shake, are sorrows of our own making. Regret is sorrow we bring on ourselves, through something we've done or not done, a decision we've made or failed to make. It is a step on the path because it entails awareness—consciousness of one's responsibility for the consequences of one's action or nonaction. There is no regret without awareness. You can't regret what you are not conscious of. This awareness is an ally on the spiritual journey.

The way to transform regret into wisdom is through spiritual practice. It entails finding out who we are on the inside and coming face-to-face with our regrets, which is probably why we resist going there. But until we know ourselves and love ourselves, we can't forgive ourselves, and forgiveness is the magic wand that releases us from regret. We need not be victims of our regrets. The ego would love that. It gets off on our sense of failure. Its favorite pastime is to yank us out of deep sleep and roll reruns of previous infractions. But when we are obsessing about our regrets, nothing is happening. We are in stasis. What's the alternative? It is to look at the *actions* we regret and receive whatever teachings they offer.

Regret will always lead us to the place where we betrayed ourselves, where we violated our own essence. Of course, we may have betrayed and hurt others in the process. But now we can transform our regretted actions by recognizing them and mourning them, forgiving ourselves and asking forgiveness of others. Beyond our acceptance and grief there is wisdom. Even regret has its place in the order of things. It is part of the chaos of being human. By traveling this path we become the avatars, those who have dared to go into the wilderness, returning to tell stories and offer rough maps for those who might follow.

Your ego is totally blind to the wisdom of the avatar, and it ain't never going to get 20/20. It's also never going to be comfortable in chaos. Why? Because it loves the security of attachments to persons, places, beliefs, and feelings—as long as they promise not to change. In short, the ego loves anything that offers stasis. It's ill fitted for a life in this universe whose creative center is moving and whose life source is chaos. The ego is a couch potato.

It's not like you should jump up and start doing for the sake of doing, or letting go for the sake of letting go. Rather you need to relax and cultivate not a vegging-out calm but an active, alive, focused calm.

Think of Gandhi, who, surrounded by chaos, said, "I have so much to accomplish today that I must meditate for two hours instead of one."

Dancing chaos is an intense form of moving meditation. It's a relentless rhythm that breaks down all barriers to our awareness. And in that divine opening into nothingness, the stillpoint at the center of our being, we find new eyes. Letting go of the known and receiving the unknown, we can sense new possibilities. When we expect change, life rarely disappoints us. In the dance we can get to know ourselves well enough to be aware of the judgments, expectations, and attachments that inevitably get in our way.

Whosoever knoweth the dance dwelleth in God.
RUMI

## cracking the code

I know all one can know when one knows nothing.
MARGUERITE DURAS

True confession: years ago I was a nicotine junkie. After a few unsuccessful attempts to quit, I decided to take a more original approach. Instead of suffering butt envy while hanging with an unreformed smoker, I would shift over to the bigger picture and see my friend as the part of me that was smoking. Thereby I could sit back and enjoy the buzz without the bad breath. I was smoking in spirit but not in body.

Intention allows you to transcend physical boundaries and transform your circumstances. A friend told me that she went to sleepaway camp in Maine when she was twelve. Every morning the girls took cold showers, and if you know Maine, you know even summer mornings aren't exactly balmy. Before stepping into the freezing water, she would psych herself up by imagining that she was stranded on a desert, sun beating down, sand scorching her feet. When she had worked up a sweat, she'd jump into the shower.

Everyone has an internal magician who can conjure up creative solutions to any situation given the intention to break out of routine thinking. Another friend told me the story of being lost in the New Mexico desert, a land of seemingly infinite distance where road markers have long ago disappeared, if they ever existed at all. He pulled over to the side of the road and meditated. The image of a raven popped into his head, and he immediately knew that this raven would show him the way. His monkey mind sarcastically commented that this wasn't a great deal of help, since Raven wasn't in the car with him. But when he came to the next intersection, not one but two ravens stood at the side of the road. Like shadows in the hot sun, they both pointed to the left. My friend turned left, figuring he had nothing to lose.

The road continued for another five miles, then ended abruptly at another T. Again the ravens were there. The same ones? Probably not, but there were two standing beside the road, this time pointing to the right. My friend turned right.

There was still one more decision to make, another crossroad, except this one presented three choices—left, right, and straight ahead. My friend looked around. No ravens this time. Just as he was about to give up, he looked up at the sky. A single raven passed over the car, banked to the right and vanished into the sky. My friend turned right, and within the next mile or two spotted the highway that would take him back to Albuquerque.

Navigating the chaos of the imaginal world with intention makes you aware of signs and symbols all around you, of coded messages that the universe provides all travelers. Sometimes, when you're really in need, a whole map will appear to describe exactly where you are going and how to get there.

It was in observing the body in motion that I received the images that eventually became the map of the 5Rhythms™. It was as if I were in a desert, like my friend in New Mexico, and signposts suddenly appeared pointing the way to return the spirit to the body. The language of my maps is rhythm—a universal language.

All maps in the imaginal world speak to that which is universal in us. They use metaphors and symbols to bypass the head to reach the mind, the ego to reach the soul. Think of astrology, the I Ching, medicine wheels, eneagrams, and the Tarot. It was intention that transformed these symbols into useable systems. Think of all the wacky dreams you've had. If it's your intention to do so, you can receive amazing guidance from them. Otherwise they remain way out, wacky, and weird.

When you are moving on a symbolic wavelength, there are no accidents. Every detail has meaning. Terry, my favorite shaman, once told me that the wind had blown several Tarot cards onto the floor just before a client walked in. Instead of just picking them up, she looked down and realized the reading had already begun. There was the card of the Devil, and there were several sword cards. It turned out the woman was having an affair with this really evil guy who was trying to control her every move. Terry told her to pick up her sword and cut the tie.

People like Terry operate 100 percent intuitively on the imaginal plane, constantly translating the profound mysteries of life and love into a language we can grasp. But we all have this ability. It's the nature of mind. They are just showing us the way to make abstract concepts relevant to our lives.

Our neural networks are like a spider's web—all parts are interconnected. It takes intention to see and interpret the connections. Once you can read the road signs, you can not only predict the direction of your life's journey but also be a creative collaborator and choose which direction you want to go. Actually, you don't even have to consciously make choices at all. If your intention is in sync with your intuition, your actions will automatically be guided from within.

Living this way takes a special kind of courage. It's not like facing shadowy figures in dark alleys; it has more to do with surrendering to the quiet wisdom of your own voice, your own ability to respond to and contribute to the moment, no matter where it takes you.

Is this guidance always infallible? Absolutely not. If it speaks to your gut, bypassing your brain box, trust it. And maybe when it's right it's not such a small voice, either. E. L. Doctorow says: "A sign is a sign . . . it is a thunderous silent thing."

# spinning the web

Could I be in Texas?

No, it could have been anywhere. Then again, it must have been nowhere. It was a place where heaven and earth come together, a place where one dream unites with another, a place where the sweet dry wind blows on forever.

BANANA YOSHIMOTO, *Amrita*

In deep silence there is no mine and no thine. Life is simply life; it is one flow.

OSHO

The truth marries no one.

SPANISH PROVERB

You knock at the door of Reality. You shake your
thought-wings, loosen your shoulders, and open.

RUMI

**O**n the edge of a cliff in Big Sur, California, from which
you can see miles of rugged coast, perches a restaurant called
Nepenthe. Sitting on the deck, munching an ambrosia burger
with fries, back in 1979, my attention was captured by a huge
sculpture of a phoenix. I'd seen it many times, but I had never
communed with it until this day. It turns out there was origi-
nally an oak tree in that place, and when it died, the sculptor
Edmund Cara transformed the carcass into a phoenix for Lolly,
who owned the property.

Part of the Nepenthe experience was cruising the adjoining
Phoenix Gift Shop. We're not talking roadside souvenirs and

snow globes here. The Phoenix is a gallery of exquisite art made by Native Americans and local artists.

Wafting through the door, I was inexorably drawn to a lonely Lakota Sioux pony drum hidden in a dark corner. It was if she had been hiding from all those trendy tourists—waiting for me. I sat right down and played her. It was love at first beat.

When I brought her home, our intimate affair became a ménage à trois. My husband became equally smitten. How we worked this out was that he played her and I danced to her song. Soon she became the inspiration for our first album, *Totem*, and the heart of all the albums that followed.

She traveled with us around the globe. In the early days, they allowed us to bring her on the plane, but later we were forced to check her as mere baggage. We never put her in a box for fear she'd be treated as any other cargo. We wanted people to know they were handling something fragile and sacred, so we checked her in "naked," with just a luggage tag dangling from her strap. She seemed to always receive respect that way.

Until one day in 1994 when we were flying from California to Arizona. Standing at the baggage claim in the bright and tidy Phoenix airport, we were shocked to see her appear crushed and broken into eight pieces. We were devastated.

That year we put out an album called *Tongues* and dedicated it to her:

This album is dedicated to
BERTHA,
our Sioux pony drum
who was murdered by an
America West baggage handler
on December 9, 1994.

Rest in the beat.

Some months later, I was looking at some of our handmade African drums and realized they were made like barrels—slats of wood glued together. I called our friend Bruce in Maine. He was a woodworker who was just getting into making drum frames. He said, "No problem. Send me the pieces and I'll glue them back together." So I shipped the pieces to Maine. A few weeks later Bruce called to tell me that all was well and he would UPS the frame back. It arrived a few days later. We eagerly opened the box only to find Bertha now in four pieces. The old breaks were perfectly mended. These breaks were new.

We sent them back to Bruce. This time he drove the drum frame down from Maine to Manhattan. A drummer friend in Brooklyn put on new skins, and we rechristened her ReBertha.

She looks different. She went from blonde to brunette. Her new skin is darker and covered in fine hair. Her tone is deeper and wiser. And she only travels by car. More than a face-lift, Bertha experienced a total resurrection, like the phoenix from the ashes.

Bertha is still the center of all our music. A wise old crone, she teaches us that falling apart is essential to achieving a higher self, one that is more resonant and responsive. Those months when her shattered body lay wrapped in a black velvet cloth in our living room, her soul had lost its voice. But her spirit remained intact, guiding us to find a way to put her back together and restore her song.

Too many of us go through life like carelessly handled baggage, battered, bruised, and broken, our souls knocked out of us. Even though we may be walking around in black velvet, acting as though we've got it all together, underneath we're in shards. We may not be physically in pieces like poor Bertha; rather our bodies, hearts, and minds are out of sync. We lack integrity. Integrity is the intuition of the soul. Without this connection to our souls, we are unable to recognize and respond to spiritual guidance that can help us piece ourselves back together.

People with integrity act in an honorable way. This may seem easy, but it's not what we were brought up to do. Superficiality is safe and sane, a good place to hide our insecurity and fear. Because deep down aren't we all afraid that someone is going to discover that we don't have our shit together, that we don't know what we're talking about, that basically we're winging it without a prayer? So, in an effort to seem in control, we act one way while another part of us is feeling quite the opposite. World War III can be going on in your head about something a friend did or said, and the phone rings, it's your friend, and you go into charming chat mode and don't even mention it. All the while feeling deeply sad and betrayed.

There is no way to think one thing, feel another, act out a third, and be in integrity. We have been raised to be dishonest emotionally and physically, our heads left to carry the weight, to figure out not what we feel but how we can mask whatever it is we feel. Not what we want to do but how not to let this desire show.

No wonder we are so dazed and confused and feel so disconnected.

Integrity is not being right or good, but being real. When you're not being true to yourself—when your own body, heart, and mind aren't in agreement—you find yourself torn by contradictory impulses, and you end up taking sides against yourself, which ultimately leaves you feeling rotten and ripped off.

Say a friend needs to borrow money. You don't have much, and what little you have you'd rather not give away. But you hear yourself say yes, and you give it. Now every time you see this person you feel resentment, but you don't mention it. You also fail to ask when your friend intends to pay it back. Soon you demote your friend to former friend and write him off along with the money.

We're desperate to communicate our real feelings, but we can't. We don't know how. We're afraid of being impolite, or hurting other people's feelings, or being considered selfish. But there is a big distinction between being true to yourself and being selfish. Being true to yourself is knowing what's going on inside you emotionally, physically, and mentally and communicating it honestly. This is what it means to give your soul voice.

Being selfish is when your ego steals the mike. Instead of speaking from love it speaks from fear of what it's going to lose or what it's going to gain or what other people might think. It speaks from the head or the heart as if they were separate. We may be feeling needy but acting self-sufficient, totally resentful but acting concerned, driven and defensive but acting laid-back and open-minded. Tempting as it may be, you can't kiss the ego off the stage, yours or anyone else's. You have to acknowledge you're stuck in your head or your heart, find your feet, and move faster than you can think or feel.

This is why we dance. When we give ourselves over completely to the beat, it aligns us, gets all the disparate parts of us in sync. When we move, we're in the moment, conscious of our bodies for better or worse. And it's in our bodies where all this mental and emotional undercurrents are happening. So the choice is yours—you can identify with a chorus of bickering energies or you can dump them all in the dance.

For twenty-five years, sweet Bertha has provided the beat for me. Every day as I do my movement practice, I listen to her song call me back to my big spirit self, my phoenix self, a self that rises above the petty concerns of my daily existence and lets me soar with the angels. When we give ourselves over completely to the spirit of the dance, it becomes a prayer. Each bead of sweat like the bead of a rosary.

After Bertha was reglued and reskinned, we threw her a re-birthday party. One of the presents she received from our dear friend Chris was a leather handle adorned with hundreds of tiny beads in different shades of blue. Chris told me that each bead was a prayer for harmony, the overall pattern representing the marriage of earth and sky. Like Bertha, when one is in harmony, in integrity, one resonates clarity. One's voice rings true and becomes an inspiration to all who hear it.

## dancing in the black hole

> We are joined together with invisible threads, If I hurt you, I hurt myself. If I hurt myself, I am hurting you all.
> OSHO

Thirty-five years ago, at a party in L.A., I met a man dressed all in black who spent the entire evening leaning against the same wall. We talked for a few minutes. Other than that he was from Santa Fe, I couldn't tell you a thing about him. And yet, more than half a lifetime later, the image of him, his presence, is as vivid and real to me as it was when I was standing two feet away from him.

People who make a strong impact on you really get under your skin, live in your body, touch your heart, infiltrate your mind. Even if you are in their sphere only briefly, they some-how splice themselves into our DNA, and you effortlessly carry them around in your cellular memories.

Memorable people are not necessarily celebrities or those who hire PR firms to imprint their images on our poor, de-fenseless psyches. Rather, they are people who are present—body, heart, and mind all connected in the here and now. People who are comfortable in their own skin, in their own emotions, with their own opinions; people who aren't constantly seeking validation, approval, or feedback; people who have faith in themselves; people who move instinctively, relate inti-mately, think imaginatively—in a word, people who are inte-grated, who live soulfully. Isn't this how we all want to be?

Your soul is the origin of your personal style—the way you walk, the way you talk, the way you walk your talk. It's when your physical, emotional, and mental energy all resonate in sync to a particular frequency. This frequency is your unique identity, not something fixed but something constantly vibrat-ing. Something moving you in the direction of your ultimate purpose, which is your spiritual path.

Contrary to many opinions, just because you have a self doesn't mean you have a soul. You might have been taught that everyone has a divine soul and its ultimate destination is out there in the stratosphere somewhere. But my experience is based on what I see here on earth. And I don't see that many earth an-gels. I see a lot of wounded people, people carrying scars big and small, myself included. Some part of us has been rendered dysfunctional through neglect, ignorance, or abuse, often by unwitting others who have experienced the same. And the wheel turns.

The result of these physical, emotional, and mental cuts, bruises, sprains, and breaks is a fragmentation of some primordial wholeness that probably started slipping through our grasp the moment we were born. But the memory of it lingers in our consciousness, and striving to reclaim this unity is the mission of our spiritual lives.

Osho says, "Only a whole man is a holy man." And to become whole again we have to find the holes in our wholeness. These are gray holes, areas of uncertainty where we aren't sure who we are or whom we are with or what our place is—unfortunately for our ego, which likes things fixed and secure. The answers to these questions change from one moment to the next. Life isn't an SAT where you just fill in a bubble with a number 2 pencil and hope for the best. You can't just say I'm a rock star or an acupuncturist or that you're with a rock star or an acupuncturist or that you are destined to be a rock star or an acupuncturist and think, "Well, that's that. I'm all figured out." We're too complex for that. In a world of constant change, we have to rely on our souls, which can spontaneously and effortlessly answer all three questions at once.

When we lack integrity, our souls can't inhabit us. They escape to divine black holes, starlight lounges for displaced souls seeking refuge from dysfunction. There they patiently wait till we get our shit together, knowing that is the very process that will allow us to rescue them. To rescue your soul, you have to dance in the black hole. This is holy work. It is the way to become a whole and holy person.

It's hard work identifying our wounds, much less healing them, and it doesn't happen overnight. Many of us do not want to go down that path, open that can of worms, dance with those demons, not realizing that it is the only way to retrieve our souls.

One of my students had the most peculiar way of dancing. His body moved, his legs moved, his feet moved—but his arms were like dead weights hanging by his side. After months of watching and waiting for him to change, I took it upon myself to bring this anomaly to his awareness. So he began to try to integrate his arms into his dance, but it was really a struggle. Allowing myself to see the pain of his struggle, a veil lifted. Hidden in his chest I saw the image of a young boy suspended by his feet. I told him, and he said, "When I was a kid, my dad used to hold me upside down over the toilet and threaten to flush me whenever he got mad." All of his fear, his rage, and his sorrow were jammed into his arms. Once he reconnected to his story, this piece of his wounding, all this energy was released. It took many dances, many journeys into the black hole, but eventually his arms found their voice and became connected to the rest of him.

Ask yourself—*Who am I? Who am I with? What is my place?* It's only when you can instinctively answer these three questions that you are moving on the soul plane. If you know who you are, you know what you need and how to be. If you know who you are with, you know what they need and how to give it to them. If you know your place, you know how to fit in and what you have to offer. Chances are at least one of these questions is driving you crazy. It is the source of your frustration and suffering, not to mention your loneliness, lack of direction, or lack of self-esteem.

My prescription for my own healing and the healing of others is to dance. Dance alone to discover who you are. Dance with others to discover who you are with. Dance in a group to discover your place. Put your psyche in motion and it will heal itself.

If you dance long and hard and deep in the black hole of your own consciousness, the power of your soul will kick in and kick butt—specifically yours. All your secret hurts and wounds, fears and failings, regrets and upsets will be swept away in the dance till eventually there's nothing left of you but the dance.

## the lone star

Many years ago, after teaching a workshop in Texas, I stayed on an extra day to give intuitive readings. My third client was a tall, heavyset man in a black cowboy hat. When he walked into the room, even the air around him seemed weighed down. My first impression was fractured—he was broken in pieces, a leg here, an arm there, his head floating, a vacuum where his heart should have been. In his lower abdomen I sensed an enormous, agonizing constriction. He was sweating profusely and wouldn't look me in the eye. It was tough getting a read on him at first, as he kept raising new defenses. Finally, words began to flow. "You have tremendous wealth, but it's all stuck in a vault in your gut. There's no movement there. It's like you are taking everything in but letting nothing out." He sheepishly confided that he'd recently had a colostomy. Until then he'd been totally unaware of this part of his body and now he felt as if something were eating him alive from inside.

There was something consuming him, but it wasn't the cancer. Instead, hundreds of images of magnificent tribal art flooded my mind. I said, "Being inside you is like being in a museum." His jaw dropped, and suddenly I felt his heart awaken. He said, "I think I need to show you something. Are you free this evening?"

Later that evening he picked me up and drove me to a nondescript suburban house. When he opened the door it became clear that no one lived there. Every room was filled floor to ceiling with artifacts, paintings, sculptures, tapestries, masks, headdresses, baskets, costumes, instruments, ritual objects. One of the bedrooms was completely filled with chests of turquoise. It was an exquisite collection, beyond description. But no one, not a neighbor, not a friend, knew it was there; just this giant, lonely, rich man with a passion for Native American art. He had been driving all over the Southwest accumulating precious objects for the past twenty years and locking them away in a suburban vault.

"This is what is eating you alive," I said. "You have to let it go or it will drag you to your grave." Moving from room to room, I was overwhelmed by the magnitude of the treasure that had been stolen from humanity. Each of these works had come from the depths of somebody's inner world in an attempt to communicate their particular vision. Trapped in this mausoleum, those voices were silenced. At the same time, I felt great compassion for this hulking man whose soul had resonated so strongly with these glorious artifacts. But like all of us, his soulful intentions were thwarted by an ego, in his case a very avaricious one, that was intent on not allowing him to share his passion with the world, to fulfill his destiny as a philanthropist. "Wow. The museum I saw inside you earlier is a dream, and the realization of that dream is your freedom," I told him.

He slowly sank to the floor and cried. As he wept I could feel him reassembling himself, his head, his heart, his belly, all heaving together in sob after sob. At last somebody had seen through his veil of secrecy and uncovered his obsession so that he could identify it and move through it.

We agreed that the only right action was for him to create a museum. With this decision I felt his soul stirring, released from its bondage at the prospect of having something to offer to this world, of finally knowing its place.

People who are soulful identify with their souls. People who are egotistical identify with their ego, that part of us that creates anxiety, insecurity, and arrogance, that constantly separates us from ourselves, each other, and the world. The ego lives in a state of constant siege, embattled, defensive, strategizing its own survival.

Your soul is born out of the unity of your body, your heart, and your mind, and it is moved by the universal spirit. Therefore, if you want to connect to the unified field, the bigger picture, you have to become unified within your own field. When your body, heart, and mind are on the same wavelength, you act with integrity. And when they're not you don't. You betray yourself. You betray others. You betray your community. When your body, heart, and mind are not in alignment, when there are gaps between how you move, feel, and think, it leaves room for your ego to weasel in and create division and conflict in your inner world and discord and discontent in your outer world.

How do we embrace a soulful, integrated existence? We embrace it by letting go of everything we are holding onto. We have physical attachments, like our daily dose of caffeine. We have emotional attachments, to feelings, to people, to pets, to place. We have mental attachments, to ideas, biases, prejudices, dogmas. The things we carry can get pretty heavy if we weigh it all in. Think of my obsessed oil man; his head was heavy with secrecy, his heart weighed with guilt, his body dragged down by centuries of Native American heritage. He had a lot of ghost dancers haunting his existence.

The soul is weightless; it carries everything and holds onto nothing. A great way to experience the difference directly is through the dance. First, move freely for ten minutes, focusing on your weight; feel how your arms hang from your shoulders, your head wobbles on your neck, your legs sink into your feet. While moving, investigate all the ways you are weighed down, from gravity to greed, from flesh to fatigue, from sorrow to sloth.

One by one, detach yourself from these sandbags and, like a hot air balloon, feel yourself rise. Breathe in your greed and let it out. Breathe in your sadness and your fatigue and let them out. For ten minutes dance as if you are weightless. It's a moving meditation, a conversation with your soul.

## homeland serenity

A candle is made to become entirely flame. In that
annihilating moment it has no shadow.
It is nothing but a tongue of light
describing a refuge.
RUMI

Flipping through *The New York Times* this morning, a story touched me unexpectedly and deeply. In Qalquilya, a town in the West Bank, Brownie, a male giraffe, died when he collapsed in terror during a burst of gunfire. Shortly thereafter, Ruti, his mate, miscarried their baby girl. The zookeeper believes that her profound sadness led to the stillbirth.

Clearly, Brownie and Ruti aren't partisan in the Mideast conflict. They are innocent bystanders, just like the millions of ordinary people caught in the crossfire. But they have a lot to teach us about the ravages of war. Even if we are not on the front lines, even if we have no opinion about the lines, we are all affected by war on an emotional and physical level. Terror, rage, and sadness permeate the air we breathe in this fragile world.

Are we doomed to passively inhale this toxic atmosphere and let it corrode us, or is there something we can do to transform it? Some of us become passive in the face of overwhelming tragedy. The images alone—a naked, dusty child with a bloated belly, a pregnant suicide bomber, a maimed Chinese factory worker—overwhelm us. It is easy to feel paralyzed in the face of fear and desperation. Alternatively, we can become galvanized by anger into an aggressive stance—shouting at the TV, pontificating at the water cooler, raging against the machine. The passives inhale, the aggressives exhale. And then there are those who just hold their breath, overwhelmed by sadness, in a dance of denial and despair.

We get caught in a cycle of passivity, aggression, or despair, and nothing changes. We think we're doing something, that we're involved, when in reality we're just spinning our own wheels. Ironically, doing nothing may be the best way to do something. Whether the war is in your head, between your legs, or between heads of state, to create peace you have to be at peace—within yourself. Sitting in silence may be the most positive action we can take to change the world. Remember Gandhi. As Osho says, "Only when there are many pools of peace, silence, understanding, will war disappear." This is my attraction to yoga.

It may sound self-indulgent: war is raging, and you are doing yoga. But cultivating a practice that opens you up to the direct experience of war and peace in your body is an honorable and even necessary way to go. The way yoga works is to create a harmonious whole by creating harmony within each individual part. In theory, this sounds great, but in practice it takes a strong commitment to reach that place of sweet surrender. Say, like me, you have a tight hip. You could take the passive approach: "My hip is too tight; I can't do that asana." Or you might choose a more aggressive tack: "Forget the hip. I'm doing this pose and I'm going to hold it longer than anyone in this room." Or you could simply create your own version of the asana and deny your hip is even involved. Each of these is an act of war against your own body.

A more productive approach would be to listen to your hip or, as my yoga teacher Rodney says, "approach it with the curiosity of a child." Is there a story it wants to tell you, a feeling it wants you to feel? In yoga we learn to be receptive to our aches and pains, to breathe in and through them, and thereby release them. "Energy flows where attention goes," says Serge King, the Hawaiian kahuna.

When you are not resisting, when you simply relax into the flow of your energy, you short-circuit your ego and create a space for your soul to emerge from the dark mysterious quiet within. However, if your surface persona is anxious, tightly wound, or filled with turbulence, your soul will retreat and remain in hiding, leaving the field wide open for an ego invasion.

The ego is the force that gets us into global messes as well as personal ones. It sees the world in black and white, good and evil, left and right. It has to be pro or con. It can never be *with*. It has to be *for* or *against*. It can never be part of it all. It can never just be. It always has to create tension and conflict. It can never let you relax and let go.

In a world of rap wars, gender wars, star wars, world wars, hip wars, head wars, heart wars, and holy wars, you need a way to access the part of you that is connected to the whole, to find a proactive way to create peace in your piece of the world. You can't have one part of you struggling against the rest of you or the many parts of you struggling against each other if you want to be fluid and free. Freedom comes when you are receptive to the voices of the oppressed, whether they be your hip, your mother, or downtrodden people. Through deep listening comes right action. As Carl Jung said, "I'd rather be whole than good."

# dancing with wolves

Ask yourself: if there were no praise and no blame, who would you be then?

QUENTIN CRISP
*Resident Alien*

It's a hot August night and I'm leading a workshop of a couple of hundred hungry souls. The room is salty, dripping with sweat, each body pulsing with primal prayers. The kind of prayers that rip you open, that erupt from your core. We've been dancing for days and nights, tracking the truth, tracking the scent of something real.

We are wolves, part of a pack yet lone and distinct, like grains of sand on a silver desert. Each reflects the moonlight in her or his original way. As the music carries us through the rhythms of our lives, we explore what gives us our unique identity, how we bring that identity to one another, and how we serve within the larger whole of the community. It is a quest that challenges each one of us to the core.

One of my students, Cora Greenhill, put it like this:

**following wolf**

In this pack I have tracked
and padded and pulled and sometimes
pounced and even
snapped
and been puzzled and paused
sniffed, twitched,
caught the drift
found a way forward
or around.
In this pack I have felt
welcomed and alone
embraced and shunned
powerful and decrepit
infant and ancient.

In this pack I have seen
fellow wolves
smelled their breaths and bodies
known
the stink of fear
pent anger and spent anger
howling grief
roars of sorrow
emptiness
bereavement
pup play
languorous joy.

In this pack I have traveled
in company
through thickets and under open skies
learning to sense
packwise.

In the wild, the wolf is a social animal; its very survival depends on instincts that honor the pack, the community. Males bond with their mates and their pups. They take part in feeding, protecting, and training their offspring. Though each animal is highly individualized, they hunt as a pack, a community, a tribe, and share in the spoils.

Wolves find the balance between separateness and unity. Even the lone wolf is part of the pack. Instead, we tend to seek one or the other, making individuality and community into an either-or proposition. Wolf knows he is both. For us humans, this wisdom is lost early on, as soon as the ego makes its debut. Later, motivated by an inner longing that we cannot even name at first, we may again seek that tribal rhythm, exploring different religions, clubs, cliques, and cults. It is a calling, one that often comes as a whisper, perhaps the result of our own minds putting words around some primal desire that is beyond our fears, beyond the language of our conscious minds. And we'll keep moving until we find that sense of belonging.

Things that are instinctive to a wolf can put a human through a lifetime of therapy. A wolf knows three things: who he is, who he is with—friend, family, foe—and what his place in the universe is. One of the reasons we struggle so with defining our separateness or togetherness is that we're trying too hard to answer these questions. Wolf doesn't sit around thinking, analyzing, agonizing. He trusts his instincts, which tell him all he needs to know, and he has an innate sense of intimacy with himself, his fellow wolves, and his environment.

When you know your place in the pack, you, too, can sit back, relax, and howl at the moon.

## black butterflies

> There are only two ways to live your life. One is as though nothing is a miracle; the other is as though everything is a miracle.
> ALBERT EINSTEIN

The movie theater around the corner from me is showing *Spider-Man* on three screens. But what about Spiderwomen? Wouldn't we all like to know more about the great mother and her awesome spider spirit, spinning her wondrous web, for while we all live in her etheric threads, only rarely do they reveal themselves to us. Our "Eureka" moments of unity or synchronicity occur when disparate parts of our lives seamlessly connect and our place in the universe is suddenly illuminated. We feel a sense of reassurance, of belonging, of being on the right path, of being nurtured by her.

To experience this, we have to be open and trustful, willing to listen and even pursue the most unlikely callings.

Immediately after the first session of a workshop I was doing in Oklahoma, a slightly built, gray-haired gentleman with horn-rimmed glasses approached me. I was desperate for a cup of Earl Grey tea, but he looked so downcast I gave him my full attention.

"I'm told you give psychic readings, and I have a real important question." He practically whispered, although we were the only ones left in the room.

"Have you posed this question to any other psychic?"

"Yes, I have."

"And what did they say?"

"She said, 'I can't answer that question but you will meet a black ballerina and she will answer it for you.'"

Being neither black nor a ballerina, I was blown away by this description. But on some odd psychic wavelength it was understandable how someone could describe me that way. For certain I am a dancer. And for certain I identify with black, from the clothes I wear to the people I love, to my dark inner images of stillness and fertile openings.

We went outside and sat on the lawn by the river. He asked me a question about his teenaged daughter. My insights seemed to lighten his load. All was going well. He relaxed. Then a black butterfly with periwinkle blue marking paused right between us in a flutter of delicate wings. The gentleman fainted. His body slumped on the lawn, and I began frantically splashing river water on his face till he came back to consciousness.

"What happened?" I asked.

"The last thing the psychic said to me was 'Do black butterflies mean anything to you?' I said, 'No.' And she said, 'They will.'"

In my workshop that afternoon, I told everyone to pose a question to themselves that only they could answer, dance till they dropped, then wait for a response. Pumping up the music, I dove into the dance and asked myself if I should go meet this woman. The answer came like a neon sign, blinking, "Go girl go!"

Of course, doing that was going to be anything but convenient. It involved canceling and rebooking my flight, juggling babysitters, finding somebody to do the opening session of a workshop, renting a car, booking a hotel, and finding my way through unfamiliar territory. Nevertheless, I dropped everything, bought a pair of shades, rented a sturdy dune buggy, and cruised out across the dust bowl.

I found my way to Enid and the correct address—a big old spacious house with front porches and huge lawns. When this sprite of a woman opened the door, I thought I had stepped into a Norman Rockwell painting. She offered me lemonade, showed me the powder room, and then led me into the dining room. She had a huge breakfront against the wall filled with Meissen figurines, crystal decanters, and exquisite tea sets. Light flooded through the windows, which overlooked a garden in full bloom. In the center of the room was a huge oak table, at the far end of which sat a crystal ball. As I took all this in, I could hear Big Bird chant inside my head, "One of these things is not like the other, one of these things does not belong."

She motioned for me to sit opposite her. "I don't take questions," she drawled, "I just tell you what I see and you can make sense out of it. Usually I see ten images."

She closed her eyes and said a prayer invoking the spirit of Jesus. After about five minutes she opened her eyes, peered into her crystal ball, and began speaking.

The first image she offered was one of a toddler in pajamas pulling puppies out from under a porch, something I later discovered was happening with my son at that very moment in Big Sur. The second was of me dancing in a church without walls, no name or denomination—my life's work, the Moving Center. In the third image she saw me walking through an airplane hangar holding hands with a man. (He asked me to marry him— wrong dude but an accurate hit!) The fourth image was of a tall, slender man in a navy blue suit, carrying a briefcase. "This is the man you will marry, but he won't show up for about five years," she offered sweetly. She was right—he turned out to be a briefcase-toting lawyer who, to this day, wears only blue. There were others, but her last image, the only one that hasn't happened yet, was of me dancing on the White House lawn.

I'm not holding my breath.

This total stranger, in the middle of nowhere, had given me a treasure map, a blueprint revealing the core structure of my inner journey. Until then I had never even seen my life as a journey, yet sitting in this stranger's house, hearing her words as she gazed into her crystal ball, I knew for certain I was on one. I also knew that it was all unfolding perfectly on schedule, in spite of my wanton efforts to sabotage it, derail it, or even get on with it. In this way, the woman behind the crystal ball was my guide, albeit not as romantic or exotic as some formidable shamanic dude with heavy warrior credentials. Nope, she was a Jesus-loving, all-American grandma, offering me footprints in the sand that I could track to find my way.

In the unified field we are never alone. We are always perfectly guided. Our bodies, hearts, and minds sing in harmony the songs of our souls. We join the universal choir and add our voices to the music of the spheres. When we tap into this universal wavelength, we achieve an organic, Zen kind of awareness rooted in the moment, rooted in trust, hovering like that black-winged butterfly in the dark unknown spaces between the lines, below the mind, in the deep dark of the body.

In the unified field, we can get glimpses of the mysterious, dark, chaotic path we tread. This requires keeping our inner eyes and ears open for the messages, the synchronicities, the signposts, never forgetting that each black butterfly speaks its own individual language. My black butterfly is not your black butterfly. The butterfly that flickers into my life today will not be the same one that flickered into my life in Oklahoma. Each moment of life offers a new language, new signs and symbols, that resonate in that specific context. Energy moves. It is impossible to pin down, impossible to box in. By living in the moment, paying attention to the dance spiraling around us, we drop deeper into everyday life and into the world of spirit that moves it.

## the fertile darkness

I wish I could show you, when you are lonely or in darkness, the astonishing Light of your own Being.
HAFIZ

You don't need to seek permission to have an inner life. It's there all the time—but you may not be. Instead you may be cramming in a morning jog, gulping down a Slimfast, writing a mental grocery list while reading your kids to sleep, or worrying about your overflowing "in box" while your coworker is baring her soul to you.

Many of us pencil in our spiritual time: 1:00 p.m. yoga class, Sunday morning service, Wednesday night kabala class, 8:00 a.m. chanting. The rest of our time is "real life." The only thing that makes these appointments "spiritual" is our intention that they be so. But we're capable of sabotaging even our best intentions. Yesterday a panting, disheveled young woman barreled past me, swatting me with her lavender yoga mat and nearly knocking me over with her gym bag, on her way to ashtanga class. I felt a bit of all of us in her—speeding up to slow down, frantically checking our Palm Pilots for a sliver of time to spend with God.

Just as we divide body from soul, we divide "real time" from "spiritual time." This dichotomy is the mother of all misconceptions. All time is spiritual time; it's up to us to honor that. And how do we honor this? By paying attention, being present in every moment. When we are really present, watching kids in a playground can be a religious experience. Cooking a meal becomes a prayer and pulling weeds a meditation.

Awhile back, I participated in a qigong workshop led by Zhixing Wang at St. Bartholomew's, a big midtown church, on a bitter New York winter day. Z talked for about twenty minutes about letting go of the mind, communicating directly with the universal consciousness, or qi field. We began bouncing in place, shaking our hands out, and then clasped our hands in front of our chests and gently released them as we allowed our arms to open to the side and then return to clasp. As we repeated this motion, we were instructed to wait for an impulse, some authentic message from within, and then to follow it. Follow it where? Follow it until we dissolved into the unified field, which could only happen by letting go of our personal boundaries.

A rocking motion began in my left shoulder, moved across my back, and down my spine to my sacrum. At this point my impulse was to stop moving and feel the tiredness that was my truth. I was totally absorbed in my inner world. Nevertheless, part of me was still aware of Z as he moved around the room working with different individuals. It dawned on me that the deeper we move within ourselves, the more clear we become and the more connected we are to all that is happening around us. As he passed by me, a fiery red Buddha appeared in a field of golden light. I had seen him before in previous meditations, so it was like meeting an old friend. He's a marker for me on my journey inward. We all have our own markers. What makes meditation so juicy is that on the way to the dark unknown, the universe provides an amazing light show.

Z told us that the unknown is more powerful than our conscious effort. All we have to do is consciously contact the unknown and then let it guide us. Easier said than done. Most of us have been educated to try to figure everything out, not sit around, however consciously, waiting for things to figure themselves out. We are bound up in our own intentions to take the initiative. "And who can untie the knot around the tiger's neck?" asked Z. We all sat there in the big blank.

"The one who tied it." He smiled.

At this point, Z was perched on a chair, a skinny Buddha in navy blue sweatpants with masses of black hair. Most of us were sitting on the floor in meditation pose, listening. He told us of a qigong master who went to a town to meet the mayor, who showed him his plans for improving the city. The master said, "You have one problem—the water in the harbor is so cold, ships can't dock there." The mayor was very surprised, as he knew the master hadn't been there long enough to even see the harbor. Then the master said, "But the reason it is so cold is there is oil underneath it." Now the mayor was truly shocked, as he knew this, but it was top-secret information.

"How did you know this?" the mayor asked the master.

"I picked it up."

If you are operating in the unified field, you are in a constant state of awareness. This goes beyond flashes of intuition; it is a way of being.

The next day, after the morning session, my friend Hans and I took Z out for lunch to Contrapunto, one of my favorite Italian haunts. The restaurant is on the second floor overlooking the traffic on Third Avenue and beyond where the harried shoppers race in and out of Bloomingdale's with bulging bags. The place was buzzing with pasta fanatics. I had cappellini with sun-dried tomatoes, garlic, jalapeños, and ricotta. Hans had leg of lamb, and Z had ravioli filled with ricotta, swimming in a sea of olive oil and herbs.

Two men were sitting at the table next to us. One raised his voice as he rehashed a conversation that had obviously angered him. His energy was heavy, brooding, and what we usually call dark. But it was really not dark at all. I was sitting with someone, Z, who was truly in the dark, and the feeling was quite different. This guy was stuck in the shadows, shoveling fettuccine into his mouth while he talked. Everything about him was unconscious. He had no realization that his voice was booming across the room like thunder. He was trapped in a moment in time, far from his body, in the shadows of his heart, out of his mind.

Z didn't seem to notice. He rested securely and peacefully in his own emptiness. He was taking a long sip of water, and I knew that every part of him was experiencing this simple act.

"So, Z, what is the essence of qigong?" I asked.

He explained that basically we go through two stages. The first is a dark stage—our vision is switched off, and there are no pictures on the screen. All is black. As you sustain your attention in this space, tune into it, and refine your perceptions, you enter the second stage. Gradually things begin to appear to you, signals, messages, information. Things become clear to you. Then, emerging from this darkness, we have a sense of light and clarity; we move out of the unknown into the known. We experience "inner vision," a vision based on our knowledge of the insubstantial level of consciousness.

What could be better than eating Italian food and talking Chinese wisdom? If this is globalization, bring it on!

Sated, we returned to the workshop. By the end of the weekend, I embraced qigong as a particularly beautiful and simple way to tune into the deeper energies of the universe. It is about returning to our original state where everything is connected and where we dissolve the boundaries between ourselves and the cosmos. All you need to do is tune in.

The bigger mind you tap into when you are fully integrated doesn't see you as separate from the rest of Creation. Any boundaries you see, any sense that you might have of being separate from all else, are illusions cooked up by your ego. Sometimes the best way to lose your ego is to find your feet.

Take a hike. Notice not just the leaves and flowers and trees but the spaces in between, for these are as much the patterns of the universe as are the physical patterns and organisms themselves. Take a walk at night under the stars and gaze up into the sky; contemplate not the stars or moon but the space that holds them all, for it is here that you will find the essence of the mystery, the home of infinity.

Nature couldn't function without emptiness, without vacuums, without negative spaces where nothing appears to be happening. Rhythm depends as much on the lull between the beats as it does on the beat itself. The world is one field of energy where everything rocks to rhythm.

So next time you're in a taxi, you're waiting for your dentist, or your HMO puts you on hold, close your eyes, feel your feet, and find God.

When darkness is at its darkest, that is the beginning of all light.
LAO-TZU

## you are one

All men dance to the tune of an invisible piper.
ALBERT EINSTEIN

There are fleeting moments on the dance floor when I am certain that the whole panorama of life on our planet is being displayed before my eyes. A woman in her thirties swirls by, and for a second I see Quan Yin's compassion in her face and in her arms. There, across the floor, a circle of five dancers, all legs and arms, on the verge of violence, appear to be negotiating a shared space, looking for a way out of conflict, like nations struggling over their turf. Now the king of the dance floor strides by, his movements genuinely regal, dominating the space. Here I see an eagle spiraling through the updrafts of a great mountain peak, there a Tibetan monk in deep meditation and prayer, over there a woman in her forties mourning her barren womb, and here an aging rice farmer cultivating his fields in the rain.

All around me, filling me, are proofs that the human spirit holds all of history, that we embody it in our muscles and bones, passing it along in our genes, its mystical currents flowing in our blood. Here we discover all that has occurred since the beginning of time, the explosion of form out of formlessness. Everything is all-so-clearly revealed in the chaos of the dance.

Is it mere coincidence that the dancing scenes on pottery and other art all but disappeared about two thousand years ago? Since then, we've done everything from ballet to break dancing but very little of the kind of ritual dancing that integrates the eternal wisdom of the cosmos, the kind we did on every important occasion for tens of thousands of years. If only we dared to explore the ecstasy of tribal dance, we might discover so much about ourselves, each other, and the world around us—and even touch those places where we are one.

Hunger for unity is an undertow. We're longing to be attuned with ourselves—to sense in our bodies the flight of the moon, the liquid rush of a deer through a forest, the quieting spirit of the tree, the shifting cycles of the seasons. We are re-discovering our ecstatic connection with the cosmos, with a higher power, a higher order we cannot even name. In this re-discovery we also recognize what we have lost. Like the Inuit grieving the disappearance of the sacred salmon, or Julia But-terfly, who lived for a year in the upper branches of a three-thousand-year-old redwood to save the tree's life, we can no longer turn our backs on Nature.

Back in the beginning, my intention was simply to help people move, to be freer and more relaxed in their bodies. But then I noticed that the more they moved, and the longer and deeper they moved, the more their emotions came alive, ani-mating their movements from a soulful place within, where they could access the power of their vulnerability, their tender-ness—a place that propelled them beyond their heads, beyond their egos, beyond what the external world was telling them to do and be.

As the beat throbs, a young man sparring with the ghost of his father touches the deep essence of his rage, and the dance that bursts out of him connects with something so big and so ancient that it would take all the sons of the world to hold it back. Right behind him is a fiery redhead, a punk-rock goddess in torn dance clothes. Her movements transform her from a street kid to a priestess of a pagan past. She's a goddess, her dance transcending crusades and dark ages, plagues and world wars, her soul tattooed by time.

Ancient sorrows and angers and fears and joys still inform our individual histories. The history of the human psyche stretches as far back as the first moments when creatures of the Earth found they could use their bodies to express the mysterious sensations that came from within them. What we urgently need is a ritualized way to return our power to the dance and for it to talk back to us as it once did, telling us things we don't yet know about ourselves and each other.

Over the years, I have witnessed thousands of dancers struggling with the invisible forces of do-and-don't-do and finally breaking through to their inner mysteries, overcoming obstacles that would inhibit their movements with partial truths and misunderstandings. In their movements they discover how their worlds have been demystified, sorted, boxed, and bound. No wonder a dancer could stand lost in the middle of a room of raging beats and be unable to make a definite move. Our internal history was short-circuited thousands of years ago, so that few of us remember the movements that once carried us deep down inside ourselves, into the darkness, to Big Mama's beat, where we become the truth. We have been turning to authorities for our answers, and now we are discovering that they, too, have forgotten the truth. History, the consciousness of all life on our planet, waits patiently in each living cell, wondering when we will open up to the infinite wisdom we each embody.

We are beginning to fill in the blank spaces and fall into ourselves. We are slowly but surely finding a way to integrate and embody all our inner wisdom. Funny thing is, it's our birthright, and it shouldn't be any more a struggle than breathing in and breathing out. But we lost it along the way. No matter; it's time to resurrect. Time to open our minds to new possibilities, give birth to more loving worlds.

Recently scientists discovered a whole new galaxy, older than our own, the cosmic equivalent of finding children older than their parents. Maybe that's what Einstein, the crowned king of chaos, meant when he said that if you go faster than the speed of light, time travels backward. Maybe one day we will meet up with ourselves.

### self portrait

It doesn't interest me if there is one God
or many gods.
I want to know if you belong or feel
abandoned.
If you know despair or can see it in others.
I want to know
if you are prepared to live in the world
with its harsh need
to change you. If you can look back
with firm eyes
saying this is where I stand. I want to know
if you know

how to melt into that fierce heat of living
falling toward
the center of your longing. I want to know
if you are willing
to live, day by day, with the consequence of love
and the bitter
unwanted passion of your sure defeat.

I have heard, in *that* fierce embrace, even
the gods speak of God.

DAVID WHYTE, *Fire in the Earth*

# all i can do is dance

You are what your deep, driving desire is.
As your desire is, so is your will.
As your will is, so is your deed.
As your deed, so is your destiny.

BRIHADARANG AKA UPANISHADS

The only people for me
are the mad ones, the ones
who are mad to live, mad to talk,
mad to be saved, desirous of
everything at the same time, the ones who never yawn or say a
common place thing, but burn, burn, burn like fabulous roman
candles exploding like spiders across the stars and in the middle you see the blue center light pop up and everybody goes
"AWWWWWW!"

JACK KEROUAC, *On the Road*

I used to have very definite notions about my life. I wanted to go
off somewhere in the Sierras and live alone with no food and
nothing to read but the clouds and the moon for days on end and
then maybe enter some kind of spiritual discipline, survive the rituals of secret initiations and emerge years later with nothing to
say, like the hero in *The Razor's Edge*.

JOHNNY DARK

## we have come to be danced

We have come to be danced
not the pretty dance
not the pretty pretty, pick me, pick me dance
but the claw our way back into the belly
of the sacred, sensual animal dance
the unhinged, unplugged cat is out of its box dance
the holding the precious moment in the palms
of our hands and feet dance.
We have come to be danced
not the jiffy booby, shake your booty for him dance
but the wring the sadness from our skin dance
the blow the chip off our shoulder dance
the slap the apology from our posture dance.
We have come to be danced
not the monkey see, monkey do dance
one, two dance like you
one, two, three dance like me dance
but the grave robber, tomb stalker
tearing scabs & scars open dance
the rub the rhythm raw against our souls dance.
We have come to be danced
not the nice invisible, self-conscious shuffle
but the matted hair flying, voodoo mama
shaman shakin' ancient bones dance

the strip us from our casings, return our wings
sharpen our claws & tongues dance
the shed dead cells and slip into
the luminous skin of love dance.
We have come to be danced
not the hold our breath and wallow in the shallow end of the floor dance
but the meeting of the trinity; the body, breath & beat dance
the shout hallelujah from the top of our thighs dance
the mother may I?
yes you may take ten giant leaps dance
the ollie ollie oxen Free Free Free dance
the everyone can come to our heaven dance.
We have come to be danced
where the kingdoms collide
in the cathedral of flesh
to burn back into the light
to unravel, to play, to fly, to pray
to root in skin sanctuary
We have come to be danced
WE HAVE COME

JEWEL, 8/2003

When I stand before God at the end of my life,
I would hope that I would not have a single bit
of talent left and I could say, "I used everything
you gave me."

ERMA BOMBECK

**d**uring spring break one year in college, driving down the
Nimitz Freeway toward San Jose on a sunny Sunday afternoon,
I suddenly noticed the other cars were making a beeline for the
exits as though they knew something I didn't. My rearview mirror reflected a black line moving toward my car like a grounded
tornado. As it got closer, it broke into two lines that zoomed
past on either side of me. About two hundred Hell's Angels in
black leather jackets with kerchiefs circling their foreheads and
stringy hair flying in the wind were streaming past my little
white Renault with the funky engine. They were a motley crew,
a snake loaded with testosterone and beer roaring down both
sides of the white line on the freeway like they owned it. I

smiled and waved and celebrated their existence in the innocent way of a young woman who still trusted anything in Levis. It didn't dawn on me to panic. And it didn't dawn on me to leave the freeway.

Sometimes you have to trust you're on the right path even when everyone else is heading for the exits.

Who doesn't want a fascinating and fabulous destiny? Who doesn't want to feel that they are on the right track, doing exactly what they are meant to be doing? Who doesn't want the perfect relationship, the perfect body, the perfect life? We all do, but don't look here for ten easy tips. My life wasn't spent on the right track. In fact, I spent some time on the wrong side of the tracks, but that's where I learned how to track, how to follow my intuition, and it's led me on a strange, serpentine journey.

On the surface it seemed random and undirected. Nevertheless, there was an underlying rhythm, an indefinable force that moved me along like a people-mover in an airport—but not in a linear way. Unconscious of striving for a particular goal or realizing a particular dream, I envied people who had those things. Well, sometimes. There was something wonderfully free about floating along on my own wave.

Call me naive, but all this time I wasn't aware that I was pregnant, carrying something much bigger than myself, a body of work, a healing process, an entire cosmology that would soon rock my world. When my 5 Rhythm practice was finally born, magi didn't shower me with gifts, but I did instinctively feel guided. Following those instincts led me on a path of healing and growth. The 5 Rhythms spoke to me in an intimate language of energy and movement. It was a language that inhabited my body, moved my heart, transformed my mind, released my soul, and ignited my spirit.

This language would never have revealed itself to me had I not needed to put food on my table and keep a roof over my head. Teaching movement was a way to earn a living and it was in helping others learn to move that I was moved. In my desperation to know myself and help others do the same, I glimpsed a new paradigm for understanding the complexities of human existence. Everything—birth and death, romances and heartbreaks, billiards and basketball, hurricanes and heat waves, religions and rock concerts—everything moves through the cycle of five rhythms: *flowing, staccato, chaos, lyrical,* and *stillness.* It may sound easy here, but it took years of sweat, surrender, and service to even begin to integrate the inspirational teachings inherent in those five rhythms.

As soon as I began sharing my discoveries, translating their abstract wisdom into concrete images and physical practices that people could experience and embody, I saw how moving the rhythms helped others to heal their broken lives and revive their souls. This was holy work for me. My life's purpose had discovered me, and it became a source of inspiration—holy water to quench not only my spiritual thirst but the thirst of all who came to drink at its well.

Inspiration is the intuition of the spirit. It's the breath of mystery moving through you, cleansing you and guiding you along the path of your destiny.

You don't have to be the Dalai Lama to have a destiny. Every life has a spiritual path. It's just a matter of falling into your own rhythm. Some people naturally fall into a flowing groove, a laid-back, easy-going momentum. Others are more staccato, moving at an uptempo pace. These are the people with five-year plans and 8:00 a.m. meetings. Others thrive on the rhythm of chaos—no sooner do they have an idea than it becomes manifest. Then it's time for the next one. These are prolific creative geniuses, people with their fingers in many pots. By contrast, those who live their lives in a lyrical mode are slightly otherworldly yet totally in tune with this one. And then there are those rare birds who, even when they are moving at full speed, emanate stillness. Think of a Buddha zooming by on a skateboard. These are rarely the people who make headlines, but their energy can last for centuries.

If you are in harmony with your rhythm, you move through life effortlessly. It's not like shit won't happen, it's just that you'll deal with it and it won't knock you off your center or take you out of your groove. It's when you resist your rhythm, when you try to swim against the current of your energy, that you begin feeling out of sync with yourself. Perhaps you feel overwhelmed, exhausted, anxious, depressed—all signs that you aren't being true to yourself. Challenges that you would have easily overcome become insurmountable.

When you fall into the shadow side of your rhythm, your ego seduces you off the path of your destiny. The ego is destined only for dead ends. Sabotage is its modus operandi. Flowing folks get trapped in their own inertia. Staccato guys get tense and rigid. Chaos divas devolve into confusion. Lyrical souls space out. And sweet still waters, although they run deep, can also freeze and become numb.

How do you resist the temptations of ego? If you don't drown out its siren song, you end up on the rocks, like Ulysses. It took him ten years to get back in his flow. I don't know about you, but I don't have that kind of time. To get out of any fix fast, I ratchet up the volume of my favorite song and follow my feet. They know the five steps that will put me back on track: be fluid, be focused, be free, be fascinated, and be fulfilled.

## rolling on a river

One's destination is never a place, but rather a new way of looking at things.

HENRY MILLER

Twenty-eight years ago, I was dancing in my all-white living room overlooking San Francisco, City of Light, when I had a vision. It was as if a thunderbolt had hit me. My body became perfectly still as images flooded my mind. Theatrical images—masks, actors, lights, sound, musicians, audience. It was a pageant, an epic like *War and Peace,* a climax of something, but at the time, I didn't know what. I described it to my friend Paulette, who had been sitting on the floor sketching me as I danced. She got all excited. We told a few theatrical friends and they got all excited too. And then reality bit. How was I going to create a major theatrical event when I was struggling to pay my rent and take care of my child on the income I made teaching dance in the Unitarian Church basement?

Life went on. Even when it didn't seem like I was actively pursuing my vision, it felt like I was going in the right direction. As Oscar Wilde said, "Faith is, I think, a bright lantern for the feet." It was the process of moving toward the vision that was important. Whether the actual theater piece was ever "produced" was the tail, not the dog.

People think their destiny is what they're going to be when they grow up—a famous actress, a diamond-dripping socialite, a Nascar superstar, or president of the United States. However, the peak of your acting career could turn out to be a Nyquil commercial, your fabulous romance might end in a custody battle, and the high point of your road experience could be chauffeuring a minivan full of screaming Little Leaguers. So it didn't turn out the way you imagined. Does that mean you failed at life? No more than if it did.

Destiny is not about success or failure. It is a process, not a destination; a path, not a pot of gold. The path itself is a dream, the map of the inner landscape of your soul, which is the part of you that has a destiny. Dreams are fluid and mysterious. They're ephemeral and can't be pinned down. And they are there to be caught, not created.

Regardless of whether you become a rock star or an admiral or a billionaire, your spiritual destiny is to become real, your true self. Destiny moves; it's a dance, not a fixed goal, a process of awakening that is driven by instinct, guided by intuition, moving in unity, sparked by imagination.

Ego, by contrast, is hooked on fixed ideas, fixed identities, fixed outcomes, even fixed fantasies. So it will cling to the notion that you have one fixed destiny. It can't mess with a moving target.

Destiny is a river. As it makes its way back to the sea, a river may carry all manner of things—sand, stones, boulders, driftwood, trash, bodies, memories, dreams, life—and few of them make the entire journey. Like a river we pick up and we let go. Like a river we have undercurrents, crosscurrents, tides, moods, shallows, and depths. Like a river we are in constant motion.

Our lives are moved by many currents, reminding us that we are not alone in determining our destiny. Moment by moment we make our plans—whether or not to go shopping today, whether or not to get married this spring, whether to become a brain surgeon or an airplane pilot, a jazz musician, a paparazzo, or a janitor. It's good to have plans—they give us a map to follow for getting to the other side of the road or the other side of our lives. But in the meantime, there's all the life that you're living between making your list and getting to the store, or choosing to go to medical school and cracking open your first skull, or deciding to be a pilot and landing your first jumbo jet.

Why not look upon ourselves and everyone around us as

superheroes in a spellbinding novel, a page-turner that keeps presenting us with new and ever more fascinating twists? We are all survivors of our own most outrageous reality TV series. Okay, so we didn't create the whole program on our own, but we took it on and acted it out, struggled through its challenges, flowed with its surprises, celebrated its downers and ecstasies—and we're still here, for better or worse.

The real meaning in your life is in the living of it. It doesn't have to add up to some huge pageant. It could be sitting around a Christmas tree with eight great-grandchildren and feeling at peace with what you've contributed to the world.

One rainy day, I was rushing into my building, struggling to find my elevator key, worrying that the elevator was still broken when the door opened to reveal a huge black man in a forest-green uniform. He was the elevator repairman.

"Can you take me up to five and back down right away?" I asked.

"Why sure, ma'am. I can do just that."

The key refused to go into the slot. I stopped, took a breath and announced: "So far, this day is not working for me. I'm hoping that yours is going better." The floor dipped and we rose together.

"But, it's *your* day," he responded. "It doesn't matter whether it's a good day or a bad day. It's your day and that's reason to celebrate it." He broke into a smile so big the elevator lit up.

"You're right. You're absolutely right," I said, running into my apartment and grabbing my umbrella while he waited. On the way down I asked him, "What's the problem with the elevator?"

"No matter. If you can fix it, fix it. If it can't be fixed, there's no problem," he said.

You never know when you are going to meet a Buddha.

Just two weeks ago, I had a reading by an intuitive healer who considers herself a channel. She certainly tuned into my program. Without knowing a thing about me, my background, or my work, she told me things that were stunningly accurate about my path. When she came to talk about the present, she began to yawn hopelessly. "You must be tired giving all those readings," I sympathized.

"No," she replied, "it's you who are tired. It's okay to stop and rest, to change direction. You are about to do a theater piece that is a culmination of your entire body of work."

Wow, what a relief to have someone else see inside my head and tell me I wasn't crazy for harboring this vision for almost thirty years. I was exhausted and ready to drop, and I'd been steadily losing faith in my ability to go the last mile on my own journey. Just like the grandmotherly intuitive who called me a black butterfly, Peggy came into my life at a time when I needed confirmation that the universe was still working for me.

It's reassuring to know you don't have to go it alone. There are people out there who can restore your flagging faith. All you have to do is be open and keep moving.

# stop the world

I have to find a way for my hands to start the concert without me.
KEITH JARRETT

For a brief period when I was sixteen I lived with the mistress of a great jazz musician. Whenever he dropped by, he'd bring friends, and they'd jam all night. Sometimes horns would fly in the air without anyone missing a note. They turned everything into music—pots, spoons, ashtrays—whatever caught their fancy in the moment. These weren't rehearsals, they were happenings, totally unscripted, improvisational—magical. I was in awe. Sometimes I just had to move, follow the notes, catch the beats—just letting the music in and letting my body spin it back out. Who knew this was my destiny?

Do we guide and therefore determine our destiny, or is it that destiny uses us, sort of the way a deep bluesy sax solo uses the back rhythms of a standup bass? I believe it's more the latter—that our destiny is the result of the connections we make between ourselves and others, and our intuitive and instinctive reactions to the world around us. Like the best jazz, it's an intimate collaboration where there is no separation between giving and receiving.

Some years ago, my son Jonathan and I were teaching a three-day workshop at a seminar center on the West Coast. The morning after the workshop, as I was leaving, I passed by two very downhearted-looking Native guys sitting on the steps. I walked past them, anxious to get my car packed and race off to catch a plane home. The looks on the faces of those two men stopped me, however, and I went back to talk with them.

"What's going on?" I asked.

It turned out they were father and son. The father was a shaman, a highly respected healer from the area. The young man explained that they had a sweat lodge on the property where they often did healing rituals for people from the community. The night before, just as they were getting started, the night guard had come down to inform them that no activities were allowed after 10:00 p.m. There had been no negotiating with the guard, so the ceremony was canceled. The son said that the payment they would have received for their work had been intended to finance their trip to the Sun Dance up north, which is a very important annual ceremony. Without this income they were now unable to go to the Sun Dance.

Heartbroken and angry for them, I immediately raced around gathering together folks from my workshop who hadn't left yet. Eventually about thirty of us met on the lawn, and I sent someone to tell the two men that there were some people who needed healing.

When they finally arrived, the men had the group form a circle on the lawn overlooking the sea. Hungry for the bones of truth, the participants watched as the old shaman laid out his bear robe, his rattle, and his smudge. He then lit up and took a long drag from his American Spirit cigarette. He sucked in the spirit captured by the smoke, held it in his lungs, and listened inwardly.

"Who is the culprit who called this healing?" He looked around the circle with a slightly mischievous grin.

The shaman's son pointed to the lady in black—me. He beckoned for me to lie down on the bear robe at the center of the circle. Then he whispered in my ear, "No one can defile your spirit. Remember the little girl in your belly. She has a dream in her hand."

He beat my body with a fan of eagle feathers, then grabbed the skin right off my bones. "Free your little girl!" he chanted in my ear, rocking me roughly into a new shape. After a few moments he was done, and I crawled back to my place at the circle.

The shaman moved from one person to another, breathing, spitting, massaging and whispering, shaking secrets out of skin as his son shook the rattle and song after song rolled across his tongue.

Jonathan was now sitting on the bear robe, spreading out his arms like wings. The old shaman dropped down on his knees and blew secrets into my son's ear, a channel for new beginnings carved of smoky breath. Fanning furiously, the shaman whacked Johnny's chest and out flew an eagle. The shaman danced around the bear robe, shouting, "Fly, fly, fly!" as the Jonathan's wings beat against the sky.

Back in the circle, a thousand years later, Jonathan knew something about himself that he had forgotten.

Soon there were five people lying in the center of the circle, lost in the sky, traveling in a trance beyond time. The shaman handed his son a red pouch filled with herbs, which he in turn placed beneath each person's nose.

When he had done his healing rituals, the shaman beckoned to Jonathan, the eagle boy, and asked him to help the travelers back to their places at the circle. This was an honor, the old shaman's recognition of Jonathan's medicine powers.

All of this happened in less than an hour, yet it became an important moment in all our lives, clearly in the stream of our destiny. Yet it was purely beyond planning, beyond direction in the usual sense. What was it that told me to pause in my hasty preparations to get my car packed to turn back and inquire about the two men sitting on the steps looking forlorn? And what was it that prompted me to take the actions I did? It was the work of inspiration, pure and simple. Much was serendipitous, no doubt about that, but there was also a guiding spirit watching over us all.

For me, destiny isn't what happens as we live from moment to moment, day to day, fatalistic and cold. It has much more to do with connections. I cannot even hope to identify all the influences that moved me that afternoon. Perhaps it was the outrage at the convention center's arbitrary rules overriding a sacred act. Perhaps it was seeing the expressions of despair in the two men's faces. Perhaps, standing on that ancient Indian burial ground, I felt the bones of the Ancestors whispering to my feet. Or perhaps it wasn't the Ancestors but the wind, or the howls of future generations, demanding respect for the holy and sacred. All seem to have been woven together to create that moment, while a willingness to be open and vulnerable allowed us all to respond intimately to each other.

Destiny is informed by unseen forces, spirits that speak to us through our instincts and intuitions, that guide us into ever deeper communion with all that is, ever was, or will be.

## threading the needle of destiny

My autobiographical humorous memoir was just rejected by my publisher and this was part of his feedback: "I don't think the central character's story hangs together."

ELIEZER SOBEL

At seven, sitting with my dear friend Eva as she was dying, an etheric silver thread, glistening and beautiful, extended from her head as she passed over. Years later, reading in ancient yoga texts, I found reference to the *aka* thread that connects the physical and spiritual bodies. Each of us has a fragile aka thread, or something like it, that holds our stories together and that gives coherence and purpose to the seemingly random pieces of our lives.

Deep in thought over a plate of chicken diablo, green beans, and mashed potatoes, I tell my husband Robert that I sense that our lives are shaped by invisible threads. A gifted trial lawyer, he never seemed to be driven by his love for the law, though he loved it. I did not see him, a gifted musician, as being compelled by his love for music, but he loves it. And while he also has a special genius as a record producer, his love for it doesn't dictate his life.

"What is that thread for you?" I ask him. "What's the theme that runs through everything you do?"

He says, "I like to get up and do whatever I do well."

He likes this answer. It expresses an important truth for him, somehow saying what it means for him to feel intimately connected with his life, that he is living his destiny. Mentally, I try it on, but it doesn't fit. The bottom line is that I'm a person who doesn't even like to get up, much less do anything, given a choice. But clearly, even though he's my soulmate and our destinies intersect, his thread just doesn't fit my needle.

When I ask friends, people in workshops, and even strangers about the threads that tie their life stories together—the themes that run through everything they do—all kinds of answers come up. A Malaysian architect tells me that for him it is nature. A designer friend tells me it is the infinite circle of life and death. A public relations wizard from London says, "It's connections." A Russian rock star says, "My thread is two things that are one for me—the beauty of pain and the knowledge of a grail." Or, more perplexed, like my friend Bruce, "I put destiny up there with God, my soul, and sexual chemistry. I really don't have a clue." I call my son. Without hesitation he says, "Walking the edge!"

Hearing his words tumbles me back in time to when he was about two years old. It was an early spring morning in Big Sur. One of my neighbors called and said, "Take a deep breath. Don't panic." He told me to look out the window at the cliffs over the ocean. A tiny, barefooted figure wearing a red T-shirt, my son, was standing on a narrow ledge high above the ocean, intently watching the surf crash over the rocks 150 feet below. I crossed the road on tiptoe, fearful of making the slightest sound. Then my neighbor and I sat watching the tiny figure on the cliff, both of us holding our breath, anxious that even the faintest whisper or sense of panic would somehow be transmitted through the morning air and startle the little boy. After ten long minutes, he finally turned, saw us watching him, and then scrambled up the trail. A few feet from me he said, "Hi Mommy," and I fainted dead away.

Reflecting on Jonathan's story taught me that for each of us there is perhaps a whole cellular history hidden in these simple statements. And for me, well, I couldn't help but think that, yes, this would surely be my fate, to be the mom of an *edgewalker!*

Some of us come up with a thread right away, but most of us struggle to tease out this mysterious filament. When I asked one friend to identify the thread of her existence she felt stunned, caught like a deer in the headlights. She unconsciously kept repeating the word "threat" instead of "thread." She was sucked into an inner vortex where she could see layers of her experience. The first layer was a fruitful, forward, progressive layer filled with zillions of ideas. "But there's another layer where I just give myself shit. It's my party pooper. I have this great idea and all I can do is curse myself for not having the money, the staff, the time."

It's hard to grasp the thread of your destiny when your ego, whether it's a party pooper or a party animal, has you tied in knots. It can be difficult, at times, to move beyond the conflicts and seeming contradictions in our lives and see that perhaps our resistance, disillusion, and even our most grandiose illusions are all part of the web. Never forget that our souls have a voice in all of this and will do their best to carry us beyond the shadow world of our ego.

There are moments, however, when the ego releases its hold and we fall into our feet and land on earth. We are grounded; but unlike a lightning rod, which draws energy from the atmosphere and channels it down into the earth, we draw energy up, through our roots, our feet, our bodies, and our minds. We become radiant like Moses on the mount. This is a moment of epiphany, of inspiration.

Virginia Woolf had this idea about "moments of being"— memories that are emblazoned on our minds when everything is perfectly clear. They're like those rare moments when a river is very calm and for an instant you can see to its depths, and then the currents pick up again and the clarity dissolves. We become liquid in these moments. We lose our sense of discrete self and feel a profound connectedness to the universe.

If you are having trouble coming up with a thread, don't worry. Kick back, hang out in the refuge of inner silence. Imagine the real you, the person you are when everything clicks and you think, feel, and act in a seamless unified flow of energy. How does that look? Feel? What gets you there? What makes you drift off course? What moves you? Be fascinated by your life, probe its mysteries. Contemplate any epiphanies or crises, moments of transcendent joy or apocalyptic loss, moments when you saw everything clearly, when the big picture of your life came into focus for a fleeting instant.

Maybe you'll want to get yourself a journal and write down your story. Destiny is in the details. Write in the third person, and you'll find yourself looking at your life as a witness. From that vantage point, you'll be able to see what you could not see immersed in it. As a witness, you are outside your story looking in. If you dare to look closely, and with compassion, you may even be able to catch a glimpse of the luminous thread that shows you how it all connects. Writing without guile can be an instrument for awakening. Like a journalist on the frontline of a great war, document your own experiences—record, embellish, muse on what you see and hear, probe your inner world and connect it always with the bigger picture, the struggle outside yourself—at the twenty-four-hour truckers' diner near your home, or in your living room while your spouse's cousins are visiting. It's just a matter of keeping your eyes open.

In everyday life, we tend to scatter our stories. We tell a piece here, another piece there, not taking the time to see how the fragments fit into the whole. You tell your grocery clerk about your broken refrigerator, your best friend hears about your anger at your lover, a stranger on an airplane hears about your dream to become an actor. But it all slips away in the wind. We need to be like Spiderwoman, who goes into herself and spins her web at the corner of a window where the morning light dances along each filament, revealing patterns complex and mysterious.

Or just ask yourself the question: "What thread connects all the stories in my life?"

Swaying to the beat of Egyptian belly dance music in the back seat of a taxi careening through the narrow, one-way streets of the West Village, I discovered my thread: intuition. My life story is strung out on the invisible thread of intuition, from instinctive flashes to intimate readings to imaginative maps and projects to embracing my own integrity and everyone else's to following inspiration as my only true guide.

Isn't it comforting to know that something ties the seemingly random and ragged pieces of our lives together in such a way that suddenly there is coherence and beauty? We may not be able to easily describe the threads that run through all our stories, at least not by words alone. But to ask these questions of ourselves and others can take us more deeply and intimately into the Mystery itself, with awe and without judgment.

If only we could drop judgment and move to a place of peace beyond struggle where there is nothing to be fixed, nothing to be changed, nothing to regret or even wish for. We would know then that we were living our destiny.

# black ray of sunshine

God guard me from the thoughts men think
In the mind alone;
He that sings a lasting song
Thinks in a marrow-bone.
YEATS

At a recent workshop, for one of our sessions, ninety of us
had to squeeze into a room that could comfortably accommo-
date forty-five. The students arrived enthusiastic, took one look
at the room, and immediately started to worry about smelling
each other's coconut hair mousse or being scrunched between
shoulders or whacked by an elbow or trampled by a runaway
sneaker. To make matters worse, there were no windows, and
the fans were on overdrive, threatening to chill us out. The cu-
mulative effect, along with untold personal concerns—jet lag,
sexual tension, unrequited love, competition, performance anxiety—threatened to squash the mood. I expected this to be a
day just to get through. But suddenly the whole thing shifted
and it turned out to be one of the more powerful sessions of
the weekend. Why? Everyone surrendered their individual shit
and let themselves be enchanted by the white Christmas lights
strung around the room and hypnotized by the spell of the
D.J.'s beats, which transformed the black box into a pulsating
womb of pure inspiration. Instead of obsessing over the lack of

space, people let go of their separateness and experienced the infinite possibilities of their oneness.

At first people move in space as if in a vacuum. Then some of them wake up and discover that it is more than this—it's a mystical matrix. They discover that air is their sustenance, feeding them, feeding us all. We breathe it in and release it; it gives us life. *When you dance,* I tell them, *think of the space around you as an invisible lover.* Celebrate it. Rather than trying to beat it into submission with flailing tense arms, gratefully surrender your body to it. When you dance, be aware of being inside the Mystery and the Mystery being inside you. Allow yourself to dissolve into your surroundings and lose all sense of where your body ends and the space around you begins. Inner and outer become a continuum as you let yourself slide beyond who you think you are.

In the book *I Am That,* a physician asks the sage Sri Nisargadatta Maharaj, "If I am free, why am I in a body?" He answers, "You are not in the body. The body is in you."

I recently watched an amazing DVD, *One Giant Leap.* It's an exploration of universal concepts that touch all of us, rooted in awesome tribal music. In the film, one of the people interviewed describes his spiritual awakening: "In my case, it happened like this. I wondered, 'Who is this guy who lives within me?' When I am sleeping, he takes care of my circulation, my chemistry, my breathing, my sugar . . . of everything. And I thought that I never knew this guy. Who is this? And then I realized that he doesn't talk when I talk. He talks when I stop talking. And he talks in terms of sensations, silence, inspiration, energy. This is his language. So I began to listen to his language. Then I found that I was only breathing and he was there. This duality, that he and I are different, began to dissolve."

Inspiration is disappearing in the rhythm of your breath and letting your breath disappear in the rhythm of your being. Like the breath, inspiration doesn't belong to you; it's just passing through you. However, the deeper you let it in, the more it will stir up, catalyze, and create changes in you. And the wisdom it lets loose in you you need to let go of, share, breathe out as an offering. Inspiration is when you become one with the dance and one with God.

As my friend Eliezer said, "Only now, in my late forties, have I relaxed into the understanding that my intuition was not necessarily that I was destined to do great things but rather that it was sensing the inner creative and magical greatness of being that we all share. And so I realize at last that I am living my destiny daily, and in order to reconnect with it, I need only inhale, knowing that whether or not I'm destined to take another in-breath is a moment-by-moment mystery and grace. All this considered, I rented a rototiller and am planting lettuce and kale this year."

Driving down the New Jersey Turnpike listening to Bruce sing "The Rising," trying to block out the endless vista of oil refineries, a phrase from a Guinness ad on a billboard caught my eye that summed up my take on inspiration: "a deep, dark, black ray of sunshine." I'll drink to that.

# dance 'til you drop

> Fearlessness is not an absence of fear. Fearlessness is standing in
> your fear with courage.
> OSHO

Astronomers tell us that the universe might last forever but
intelligent life might not. On the other hand, there's a possibility
that all the planets will get sucked into an ever-widening
black hole and disappear in the vacuum, never to be seen again.
In either case, I figure developing this intuitive stuff prepares
us well for the End of Everything. At least we'll know when it's
coming.

One of the reasons people are hesitant to develop their intuition
is that they are afraid to know death—their own or someone
else's. They want selective intuition, to know what numbers
to play to win the Lotto, when they'll meet Mr. Right—good
stuff. It's like wanting to eat a pint of Häagen-Dazs without
having to consider the fat. Sorry, olestra was pulled off the
market. There ain't no free lunch.

To embrace life, you have to embrace death. It's like breathing;
you can't inhale without exhaling. It's what you do with the
knowledge that death is the ultimate destiny that can transform
it into service, into a prayer, into a dance worthy of Shiva, Lord
of the Dance, Creator and Destroyer of all things.

For example, when I got the gut instinct about my roommate not going on her blind date, I was tormented by feelings of responsibility. In the case of the Esalen doctor, I was racked with guilt—could I have stopped his car from going off the cliff? It eventually dawned on me that intuitive knowledge didn't make me responsible for intervening in a person's destiny. Rather, it illuminated the role I was meant to play in that destiny. I couldn't save my roommate, but I could comfort her mother. I couldn't save the Esalen doctor, but I could sit with him during his coma, hold his hand, speak to his heart and ease his transition between worlds.

Shortly after the doctor died, I went to do a reading for an acquaintance in Big Sur. Nobody answered the door, so I let myself in. She called to me from the bathroom. From the bathroom doorway, I could see her body fully exposed in the tub. Her body was filled with cancer from her neck to her pelvic bone. She smiled at me, completely unaware of this, and apologized for not being ready.

"That's okay," I said. "I was just coming by to tell you I can't do it today." Totally freaked, I left and went to a ridge overlooking the ocean to breathe her death in and out with the salty air. There was no way to give her a reading, pretending she had a future when she didn't. Nor was it appropriate for me to be the bearer of this news. Instead I called her ex-husband, a friend, and he took her to the doctor, where she was diagnosed. She died six weeks later.

Letting go is simply a dance. Intuition is seeing the big picture, but if we are in denial about death, it's as if we have blinders on. It's like watching a movie but only being able to see half of the screen. If we're in denial about our own death, then we can't help anybody else go through theirs. I went to visit a friend who was terminally ill. I held her hand and asked her how she felt about dying. She burst into tears, and I was afraid that I had shattered her. However, she said, "Thank God. You're the first person to mention the word. Everyone else puts on their happy face and tells me I'm getting better as they pump wheatgrass in and out of every orifice of my body. I know I'm dying and all I want is a hamburger and nobody will give me one." So I went out and got her one.

If life is the ultimate chaos, then death is its stillpoint. In the documentary film *Rivers and Tides*, Andy Goldsworthy contemplates his ice sculpture illumined by the sun and mutters: "Its life is the thing that causes its death." We need to learn to live with death, whether it be the death of a pet, the death of a person, the death of an ice sculpture, or the death of a dream. Otherwise it stalks us, imprisons us in a cage of fear and gives the only key to the ego.

For in the end it all comes down to the internal battle between ego and soul. What motivates ego to define, to hide, to diminish, to separate, and to sabotage is ultimately its fear of death. Not just physical death but the death of a relationship, a job, a hairstyle—anything that involves letting go and moving on. The ego would be perfectly happy in a wax museum, where kings and queens and rock stars and politicians hold eternal, immovable court.

The only way to thwart the ego is to outwit it; to be aware of its many voices and how they zoom around your head; to make fun of it, for it can't stand to be laughed at; and, most important, to drown it out with the beat and dance until you drop. Dance 'til there's nothing left.

I hate to contradict Christopher Plummer, who, in *The Sound of Music*, sings "Nothing comes from nothing." In fact, everything comes from nothing. The stillpoint is the source of all creativity and compassion, yet it is pure emptiness. It is the hole in us that is holy, that makes us whole. It is the pure air that feeds the spark of inspiration into a brilliant flame.

Inspiration catalyzes transformation, whether it's transforming a block of clay into sculpture, improvisations into symphonies, or the contents of your vegetable drawer into a nourishing soup. It is the creative spark that ignites a work of art, a garden, or a relationship. But as with Shiva, who embodies both creation and destruction, the spirit contains both inspiration and expiration, the breath of life and the dance of death. To deny death is to sever the spirit, to suffocate the soul.

The blessing of inspiration is the beauty of death. It's the ultimate leap of faith to hold death in an honorable way and let go of your most powerful attachment of all—the attachment to life.

Do not stand at my grave and weep,
I am not there, I do not sleep.

I am a thousand winds that blow.
I am a diamond glint on snow.

I am the sunlight on ripened grain.
I am the gentle autum rain.

When you wake in the morning hush,
I am the swift, uplifting rush
Of quiet birds in circling flight.
I am the soft starlight at night.

Do not stand at my grave and weep.
I am not there I do not sleep.
Do not stand at my grave and cry.
I am not there, I did not die.

MARY F. FRYE

## falling stars

> Be near me when my light is low . . .
> and all the wheels of being slow.
> ALFRED LORD TENNYSON, *In Memoriam*

In the days after the destruction of the World Trade Center, I was numb. All of New York City and much of the world was numb. The magnitude of the loss, the personal and collective tragedy, was too much to even begin to accept, much less integrate into our perceptions of the world. It did not seem that life could ever return to anything even approaching normalcy, for everything that once defined normalcy was gone forever. And then something shifted. A few days after the bombing, I recorded the following in my journal:

*September 15, 2001*

*Everything below Fourteenth Street is shut down. Lower Manhattan feels like an abandoned mall, sky filled with sorrow and smoke. Stunned people move in slow motion through the streets and along the sidewalks. Glued to our TV sets, channel surfing for information, for something to make sense of all this, for something to hold onto while the world we have known falls apart. The governor of New York is crying on TV, lots of men are crying on TV. My friend Terry calls. In a reverent tone she says, "We are breathing in the dead." Devastated, I stumble into the kitchen, looking for a graham cracker like the ones they gave us in kindergarten with a small carton of milk after our naps. There is nothing like that in my cupboards. Then I hear music, as if from a dream. I haven't heard anything but sirens and newscasters for two days.*

*The music is coming from the street outside my window . . . I lean out and see a group of maybe twenty young black teenagers in royal blue band uniforms with yellow tassels, a drum and bugle corps marching down the deserted street playing "God Bless America." Their music was an invocation, filling the streets, calling us to momentarily take refuge in the rhythm. They were like warriors delivering us from the shock and horror back into the vital beat of our hearts. And it occurs to me that they were brought together in this moment not just by grief or fear or music——though all of these play a part——but by an instinctive realization and excitement about their unique contribution to this moment. We needed them. They heard.*

As I watched and listened from my window, the little band marched straight into my heart, filling me until I broke and wept. The leaden veil that had fallen over me was suddenly lifted. It hurt to feel. On the city streets in the days afterward, the same pain, the same struggles, shaped the faces of everyone around me. Coming alive again, leaving the protective veil of numbness, meant feeling our grief, our horror, and our rage. At the same time, from deep inside, came a profound sadness for humankind, for all of us, a sadness that somehow carried me beyond frozen anguish back to wonder and awe and intimacy. The band of young men marching down the street playing "God Bless America" had delivered me back into my humanness. It is in these moments of deep communion, when we recognize we have something to give and something to receive, that we embody all the teachings, all the weavings, all the strands of stories that inform who we are. As Lousie Erdrich writes, "What is the whole of our existence but the sound of an appalling love."

The day after the World Trade Center disaster, a friend of mine was cleaning a desk drawer, and a postcard fell out. He had received it from a genius puppet artist named Robby who died more than fifteen years ago. On the picture side is an image of the lobby of the World Trade Center, with the elevators side-by-side-by-side-by-side, and in front of them are ghost-like figures, feet bare, heads shaved. The one in the center of the image is looking directly at you, and it looks just like Robby. On the other side of the postcard is the title "Trade

Center" and a postmark from 1977, the year the Towers were opened. In Robby's handwriting is the following quotation:

> Let it be for you a great and high mystery in the light of nature that a thing can completely lose and forfeit its form and shape, only to arise subsequently out of nothing and become something whose potency and virtue is far nobler than what it was at the beginning.
> PARACELSUS

It was as if Robby had seen the future, his own and that of his city. Life is so mysterious.

We spend much of our lives creating containers—forms, vocations, belief systems, ambitions, and explanations for why we are here—but they are only containers. When those containers are crushed, which they inevitably will be, we discover something that endures beyond them—the human heart, the soul, the Mystery, the instinct to embrace our Source unconditionally. And so it is ultimately here, exulting in the bond and inspiration of life itself, that we intuit our own spiritual path and find our destiny.

resources

For further information about the lectures, workshops, trainings and performances of Gabrielle Roth, contact:

**THE MOVING CENTER**
**PO Box 271, Cooper Station**
**New York, NY 10276**
**212-695-4070**
**e-mail: ravenrec@panix.com**
**http://gabrielleroth.com**

Gabrielle's work can also be explored through the following media.

## videos

THE WAVE: ECSTATIC DANCE FOR BODY AND SOUL
The revolutionary moving meditation that first brought Gabrielle's work into the home.

THE POWER WAVE.
A high-velocity trance/dance workout to put your psyche in motion for self-healing and transformation.

THE INNER WAVE.
A moving meditation based in the rhythm of stillness that uses every part of your body in a "living prayer."

I DANCE THE BODY ELECTRIC.
Gabrielle in warm and spirited conversation about her unique approach to healing through the creative process and living life as art.

## albums

ENDLESS WAVE: VOL. 2
Track I: The soundtrack of *Power Wave*, Gabrielle's hot, intense video workout set to the music of the album *Tribe*, by Gabrielle Roth and The Mirrors. Voice-over by Gabrielle.

Track 2: The soundtrack of *The Inner Wave*, Gabrielle's meditative video featuring the rhythm of stillness. Voice-over by Gabrielle.

ENDLESS WAVE: VOL. 1.
Track 1: The soundtrack of Gabrielle's extraordinary video *The Wave*. Gabrielle guides you through the body parts and *5 Rhythms*.

Track 2: An unguided tour through the body parts and *5 Rhythms* set to a hot, new percussion track.

## books

SWEAT YOUR PRAYERS (Tarcher/Putnam, 1998).
An exciting rhythm ride to call the spirit back into the body.

MAPS TO ECSTASY (New World Library, 1998).
Gabrielle's internationally acclaimed first book about her work.

# music albums by gabrielle roth and the mirrors:

SHAKTI.
This compilation (featuring Bhagavan Das, Jai Uttal, Deva Premal, and others) offers an extraordinary journey of listening and healing as masterful musicians evoke, celebrate, and sing to the spirit of the ecstatic longing for the divine.

MUSIC FOR SLOW FLOW YOGA; 2 VOLS.
This compilation contains smoothly rolling rhythms that are as limber, graceful, conducive to stretching, and soul-inspiring as a perfectly formed yoga posture.

BARDO.
This second offering of Gabrielle and Boris Grebenshikov weaves transcendental, hypnotic music with a mystical language of the soul. Special guest appearance by Deva Premal and Miten.

TRIBE.
Drums, bass, percussion, and extraordinary vocals—this album is jumpin'. Great for dancing and listening.

SUNDARI: A JIVAMUKTI YOGA CLASS.
This one-hour class, set to the tribal music of Raven Recording, contains an instructional diagram for the 21 postures that will get

you into the beat of a bare-bones Jivamukti yoga class. Suitable for all practitioners. This is a compilation of music by Gabrielle Roth and the Mirrors (featuring Jai Uttal) and Chloe Goodchild. There is no voice-over on this album—it is excellent for listening, movement, massage, and meditation.

REFUGE.
Take the world beat percussion and music of Gabrielle Roth and the Mirrors; add Tibetan Buddhist chants sung by the legendary Russian rocker, Boris Grebenshikov; seek Refuge.

ZONE UNKNOWN.
Hot, driving, and trance-y.

STILLPOINT (A COMPILATION).
A collection of Gabrielle's previously released songs of *stillness*—great for massage, meditation, and yoga.

TONGUES.
A lyrical, upbeat journey through the rhythms.

LUNA (NOMINATED FOR AN INDIE IN 1994).
Deep songs that evoke the feminine mysteries—emphasis on *flowing*.

TRANCE.
Three warmup songs lead to the *5 Rhythms*.

WAVES.
High energy, with a focus on *staccato* and *chaos*.

RITUAL.

Relaxing and inspirational with emphasis on the rhythms of *stillness* and *flowing*.

BONES.

Hymns to the sacred animal spirits—one warmup song leads to the *5 Rhythms*.

INITIATION.

Side 1: A journey through the *5 Rhythms*. Side 2: A musical guide through each of the body parts.

TOTEM.

Gabrielle's oldest and most popular; shamanic drumming and trance/ dance music.

permissions

From *The Hermetic and Alchemical Writings of Paracelsus,* edited by Arthur Edward Waite (Holmes Publishing Group).

From *Shock Treatment,* by Karen Finley (City Lights Books), © 1990 Karen Finley. Reprinted by permission of City Lights Books.

From *City of God,* by E. L. Doctorow (Random House Inc), © 2000 E. L. Doctorow.

From *The Illuminated Rumi,* by Coleman Barks & Michael Green (Broadway Books), © 1997 Coleman Barks & Michael Green. Reprinted by permission of the author.